LIFE POINTS

25 DIRECTIVES THAT WILL CHANGE THE WAY YOU LIVE

DR. STEVEN A. JIRGAL

Published by The Core Media Group, Inc.

©2010 by Steven A. Jirgal

www.stevejirgal.com

The Core Media Group, Inc.

P.O. Box 2037

Indian Trail, NC 28079

Visit our websites:

www.thecoremediagroup.com

www.sportsspectrum.com

CONTENTS

DEDICATION

To our three children, Joshua, Caleb, and Sarah: May the directives and illustrations in this book help you to make the right choices and empower you to live rightly. And to my wife Pam, thank you for being such a strong anchor, encouraging and instructing by word and by example.

Introduction

Just as there are certain principles that must be employed in order for a rocket ship to leave the ground and reach its destination, so there are certain principles that must be employed in our lives if we are to reach the destination we desire. One of the most important pieces in the launching puzzle at Cape Canaveral is the launching pad. It may go unnoticed, but without a proper launching pad, the rocket ship will not be able to do what it needs to do when lifting off from earth. In Cape Canaveral the rocket sits on a launching pad that is a 60-foot concrete cube. It is sixty feet wide, sixty feet long, and sixty feet deep. A strong base is necessary in order for the rocket ship to be able to press against an immovable object and lift itself off the ground.

This is similar to the base that you and I must establish in our lives to lift us off the ground in order to reach the destination we desire. When the base is established and the rocket is placed in position for lift-off, the first thing that must be overcome is gravity. Overcoming the pull of the earth and establishing momentum are some of the most difficult parts of launching a rocket ship. In fact, up to half the fuel that is incased in the rocket is burned off in warming up the engines and moving the rocket ship just six inches off the ground. When the rocket clears the atmosphere, it takes very little effort to move through space. Little puffs from the engine move it and correct its path as it journeys to its destination.

That is also true in our own lives. It takes a tremendous amount of effort to get any program started, whether it's a business, a relationship, a club or sports team. Getting things started uses great amounts of energy just to establish the inertia needed to overcome life's gravity.

What you are about to read are twenty-five principles that will help you get off the ground and launch you to where you want to be successfully. If you will take the time to really study these principles and bring them into your own life, making them habits, then you'll be able to succeed in getting to where you want to be.

Directive 1—
Do It Now! Make Progress by Actions, not Intentions

The world is full of people who talk about all the great ideas they have and all the great plans they are making but never enact those plans. It's the great business plan, the home they are going to build, the trip they are going to take, the adventure they are going to establish, or the new habits they are going to implement in their lives. They talk about them, but they never seem to get to the point where they work through their plans and make them happen. They are people who constantly load the gun but never pull the trigger. My question is always the same: if it is such a great idea and they think it will be wonderful to do it, why are they not putting it into play? What is it that is keeping them from moving ahead with their plans?

In the movie Cocktail, Tom Cruise is interested in starting his own bar. He understands he needs help because he knows nothing about business. To remedy this, he enrolls in a business class at the university so he can start this new venture. While he is in class, he hears the theory that the professor is espousing about business and all the ways people should run a business, and it occurs to him, *"Why is this professor who knows so much about business not in business, or if he is in business, why isn't he in a successful business?"* So he raises the question, "if all these ideas are true and right and good and they should be implemented, how come you're not doing any of those?"

Those are the types of ideas or questions I have when somebody comes to me with a great idea or adventure he feels I should be involved in. There is a saying, "talk is cheap except on the cell phone." Many times these people will come and share with me the idea that someday they are going to do something. Someday they are going to make something happen. Someday they are going to... Today is someday. If you are going to make progress in your life, you have to push the button that launches your life into your someday. Today is the day you need to step up and do what you're called to do, what you're equipped to do.

Years ago John Denver recorded the song *Country Roads*. It hit the charts and went world-wide. It's just one of those good sing a long songs that's easy to follow. It's simply a feel good song. There is an important meaning in a verse in that song that you might miss if you don't pay attention. It says, "I hear her voice in the morning as she calls me; the radio reminds me of my home far away and travelin' down that road I get the feeling that I should have been home yesterday-yesterday."

Don't join the masses of people who go through their entire life looking backwards saying, "If only I had done this. If only I had come up with a good plan and acted on my plan. If only I had taken the time to get with the right people who could have launched me into this venture. If only I done the things that set me up to be in a better position I'm in." Today resist the temptation to be with that crowd. The only way to miss that is to enact a plan in your life. Margaret Thatcher once said, "No one would remember the Good Samaritan if he only had good intentions."

Generally, you can characterize people into one of three groups. The first group is the indifferent group. They go with the flow. They don't make things happen. They just see what's going to happen in their life and just sort of follow along. They follow the crowd and let the crowd decide how they're going to live and what they are going to do. They don't draw attention to themselves, they don't solve problems, and they don't make waves. In fact, you'll find that they don't make much of anything. They just live their lives one day at a time, making decisions as they come along.

The second group is the reactive type. They are highly energized, but they live their life from the prospective of waiting for life to deliver the pitch and decide whether or not they are going to swing. They tend to procrastinate and avoid having to make any big decisions. They are not risk takers, but are reactors.

The third type of person is the one that I hope that you'll become. This is the proactive type of person. They are the go-getters. They are people of action. They don't watch things happen, and they don't wonder what happened. These are the people that make things happen. They don't procrastinate, but get on the job. They develop adventures in their life and learn from their mistakes. They grow and become bigger. They launch their lives in such a way that they understand that they are the catalysts to making good things occur in their lives. One characteristic of this type of person is that they generally have some wonderful stories to tell of mistakes they have made but also successes they've had. These are the people that others want to latch on to and go along for the ride because they know it's going to be a good adventure. Proactive people know that their life is blasting off in the right direction.

So what are you going to do about what happens in your life? Are you just going to go with the flow? Are you going to be reactive and see what happens? Or are you going to be proactive? I want to encourage you to take the initiative in your life to make something happen, to make something of yourself. Give yourself an adventure. Organize those photos. Put out that resume. Tell someone you love him. Extend forgiveness. Host a garage sale. Read or write that book. Hike that mountain. Take that class. Do something! If you're going to make progress in your life, it is not going to come through an intention, but through action.

NOTABLE QUOTABLE: "FAR BETTER IT IS TO DARE MIGHTY THINGS, TO WIN GLORIOUS TRIUMPHS EVEN THOUGH CHECKERED BY FAILURE, THAN TO TAKE RANK WITH THOSE POOR SPIRITS WHO NEITHER ENJOY MUCH NOR SUFFER MUCH, BECAUSE THEY LIVE IN THE GRAY TWILIGHT THAT KNOWS NEITHER VICTORY NOR DEFEAT." THEODORE ROOSEVELT

Directive 2 —
Build Memories Not Monuments

There is a humorous illustration about a man who was a miser. He believed that money would make him happy. People told him, "You can't take it with you." But his counter was always, "If I can't take it with me, I don't want to go." He became obsessed with the idea of taking his money with him. So he made arrangements with his wife. He said, "When I die I want you to put me in a suit with lots of pockets on the front and inside, and I want you to take a certain amount of money and exchange it into gold coins. I want you to fill those pockets with gold coins. I am determined to take my money with me. Sure enough, as time went by he died. His wife honored his wishes and dressed him in his specially made suit. When he arrived in heaven, he looked down and immediately noticed that he was wearing his suit and all the pockets were filled with gold. He was so excited because he was right and everyone else was wrong. You can take it with you. He began approaching everyone he could find showing them his coins and saying, "I did it! I did it! I took it with me. Look at this! Look at this!" Look at this!" Two of the saints looked over at him and one said to the other, "Hey! Who's the new guy, running around with that road pavement in his pockets?"

I have presided over many funerals through the years, and I've observed that in that setting what we talk about is not a person's things. We don't talk about their business. We don't talk about how much money they had and how big the building was that they built. What we talk about is people. What the family wants me to convey to those who have come to pay honor to this person is the stories, the adventures, the opportunities, and the things they have gone through and overcome in their life. They are not interested in people understanding that the deceased was wealthy. They're interested in those attending knowing that the person who died was loved. It's about memories not monuments.

One day you and I will face a test and the test is not how we made the business work or how we developed ourselves into a success. The test I'm referring to may be called "the dorm test." If you have children one day, your goal might be to send them off to college. If you're able to realize that goal and they do attend college, there will come a time when they will sit around the dorm and talk with their friends about home. You will pass or fail the dorm test based on what your child says of the memories they have collected while living in your home all those years. When they bring their friends home, you know they want them to enjoy time with those who have built great memories.

There is vast different between being wealthy and being rich. When you're rich you have lots of money, but when you're wealthy, you have lots of memories. So often we spend so much time earning our salt that we forget about our sugar. But as Howard Hendricks of Dallas Theological Seminary states, "Succeeding in business and failing at home is a cop out. For no success is the workplace will ever make up for failure at home."

Recently a friend of mine told me of an opportunity he had to enter into a new business venture. It was a-once-in-a-life -time opportunity. He was going to make lots of money. But it meant that he would have to be in a foreign country for at least a year or possible a year and a half. He has a wife and four boys at home, and I shared with him that he would never gain back that time with his boys and with his wife. They would be a year older when he returned, and his influence in the home and being around those boys, shaping their personalities and future, would never come again. There were lots of people around him who said, "Go! Go! It's too great an opportunity to turn down." But I stood firm in telling him I wouldn't give up a year or a year and a half with my wife and children no matter how much money they dangled in front of me. Thankfully he didn't go, and now he is certain that it was the right decision for him and his family.

Establishing memories in your home with your family takes at least as great a commitment as building monuments. But you've got to be willing to make that commitment if you're going to build the memories that will last beyond your years. Memories come from laughter, time together, overcoming obstacles, and investing in your mate and your children.

In our home we are deeply committed to the memories we can build while our children are in our charge and under our roof. One evening we were sitting around our dinner table talking about the poetry our ten-year-old was reading. She and I had read some poetry books and just enjoyed laughing about them. Some of them had deep meaning and some were nonsense. So after dinner my daughter asked me, "Daddy do you know any poetry?" So I rattled off a little limerick that I just made up. She thought it was great and asked for another one. I began making up these simple little rhymes and I shared them with her. Well, that night I began thinking, *since my daughter loves poetry, wouldn't she cherish a book of poems from her dad?* I started getting serious about teaching her lessons through poetry. I began writing these poems down with a plan to put them in a collection and give it to her for Christmas in book form. Then it occurred to me how special it would be to illustrate these poems. I'm not an illustrator. I can't draw, and I don't have an artistic bone in my body. So I made a call to a friend of mine who is the President of the University in our area and asked if I could take an art class for free. He gave me the clearance, and I enrolled that fall in an art class. I spent that fall learning how to draw and that Christmas morning she received a gift of poetry from her dad fully illustrated and bound. My boys each received a spiritual picture that they have on their walls to this day.

It takes time, energy, effort, and might even take some money, but you have to fight each step of the way to establish memories in your home. In our home we have a game room above my shop. We built this so we could have the children home, so that the kids from the neighborhood would come to our home. We know what goes on in our home, and we've determined to be the influencers on our children and those who visit. One night, before the air conditioning was put in the building, my wife Pam and I were on the deck chatting. The window was open to the game room and we heard all the laughter coming out of that room. Pam looked at me and said, "Building that room was a great decision."

I grew up in a lower middle class family. We didn't have much, and we didn't have many extras. That didn't matter because everyone around us was in the same socioeconomic situation. Growing up we only took two vacations in our entire lives. One was a camping trip and the other one was to a lodge in the northern part of New York. But without question there were great memories established in our home. We built things, sang songs, made projects, constructed forts, and had hobbies. All of these activities bring about great memories of growing up. We didn't have a lot of things but we had memories we could tuck away and carry with us into the future. A lot of establishing memories comes down to developing individual experiences with your children. You've got to find out what excites them, what they enjoy doing, what they see as fun, and then with the creativity that you use at work, apply it to an experience with your children. Simply transfer the energy you use to fill your wallet and place it into your home to fill the memory banks of your children.

Recently a woman shared with me that her daughter talked about the upcoming Christmas holiday and asked if the boys would be home for vacation and was told they would. This young lady got very excited and asked, "Mom, can we all sleep in the living room because that's my favorite part of Christmas." This mom didn't realize that a memory was established in her daughter's life, and she really enjoyed that part with the entire family, simply sleeping in sleeping bags and in chairs all around the Christmas tree. She highly valued that feeling of waking up and seeing her family all around her.

In our home we developed something called the big ten. I asked each of our children to come up with ten memories or adventures they wanted to build as a family. I had to caution them that they were not to write something down that was simple and easy like going out to dinner, going to the movies, or traveling to the mountains. I wanted them to come up with great ideas, things that would be so big that they couldn't help but develop into great memories. The children got busy working on that. Some of their ideas overlapped so we wound up with a list of twenty-six events that need to take place that will deeply establish memories in the lives of our children. My job, even as I write this is to make those memories come true. Several of those have already been fulfilled, and they have those in their memory banks. The others are currently in process.

While you're developing these memories in your children's lives, do not forget the life of your husband or wife. Keep in mind they are the person you committed to grow old with and develop a commitment to build memories in their lives. Your children will see memories you are building with your spouse and that will in fact blend into their memory banks also. Filling the memories with your mate and with your children is a great way to establish a platform on which to grow old.

NOTABLE QUOTABLE: "THE WORK WILL WAIT WHILE YOU SHOW THE CHILD THE RAINBOW, BUT THE RAINBOW WON'T WAIT WHILE YOU DO THE WORK."
PATRICIA CLAFFORD

DIRECTIVE 3 —
OVERCOME A WORTHWHILE OBSTACLE

When you were a child, perhaps you grew up the way I did where there were certain challenges that were brought your way by those with whom you played. When you had a challenge you had to step up and meet that challenge. Otherwise you risked losing face in front of your friends. The greatest way to challenge somebody was to name the obstacle and then to dare him. The greatest dare you could give them was not just, "I dare you" and not just, "I double dare you." The greatest challenge was communicated by the words, "I double-dog-dare-you." That was the highest challenge that any young man has ever risen to in his entire life, and you can be sure that the obstacle was a large one. But be just as assured that if you ever overcame that challenge, you would at least for a short period of time be a hero to all your friends.

When you rise to a challenge even today, it leads to the fuel that moves you through life. It leads to something called empowerment. It not only empowers you as it builds momentum in your life, but it empowers others also.

At one point in the history of long distance running, it was believed to be physically impossible for man to run under four minutes in the mile. No one could do it. People had come close, and many looked like they were going to do it, but nobody achieved the sub four-minute mile until Roger Banister came along. Roger Banister was the first man to run a sub four-minute mile and within just a few months, dozens of men overcame the sub four-minute mile barrier. Once he had done it, he empowered others to see that they could do it too.

I grew up in an environment where I consistently let

obstacles stop me. If I was told I could do it, I believed that. If I was told that something was too hard, I believed that. But, somewhere around my junior year in high school I stopped listening to the voices in my head and the people around me, and I started doing the talking. From that point on I decided I was going to excel in everything that I did. I began to fill out and progress athletically, academically, and financially. It's not that I have any unusual gifts. As was mentioned before, I'm not from a wealthy family. I am not in the media eye. I don't come from a professional athletic background. Yet, one of the greatest things I enjoy is having an obstacle placed in front of me and somebody telling me it can't be done.

In college I had to take a class in aquatics. I was not a big swimmer. My biggest problem was caused by a low percentage of body fat. Because of that I really had trouble floating. But the class was required, and I failed the water safety instructor part of the course. I passed the class, but I failed that particular aspect. And this failure bothered me all through the rest of my junior and senior years in college. I was bothered by the fact that I failed a part of the class, and I carried that with me through graduation and the following two years of my life. Then I decided I was going to do something about it. Three years after I graduated I began swimming again. I enlisted the help of a coach who told me I needed to change my stroke because I was using a sprinter's stroke for a distance race. So I changed my stroke and began practicing. I would spend time in ponds and in lakes and in pools, and I forced myself to swim farther and farther. Then came the challenge that I presented to myself. I wanted to swim across the widest part of the Hudson River. It was two and a half miles across. One Saturday morning I got up early and joined a couple of friends in a boat. After crossing the Hudson in the boat, I got in the water and began swimming. I fought the waves and the current, and about 3 hours later I crossed to the other side. I will never forget the great feeling of knowing that not only did I overcome an obstacle, but I had also overcome an obstacle that had defeated me before. The water didn't change, but the swimmer did.

So much of overcoming obstacles involves the mental side of things. An anonymous writer has penned:

> As you think you travel, as you love you attract.
> You are today where yesterday's thoughts brought you.
> You'll be tomorrow, where today's thoughts take you.
> You cannot escape the results of your thoughts.
> You can endure and learn, you can accept and be glad.
> You will realize the vision, not the idle wish of your heart,
> Be that vision base, or beautiful, or a mixture of both.
> For you will always gravitate towards that which you secretly most love.
> In your hand will be placed the exact results of your thoughts.
> You will receive that which you earn, no more, no less.
> Whatever your environment and circumstances may be
> You will fall, remain, or rise, with your thoughts
> Your wisdom, your ideals.
> You will become as small as your controlling desires
> And as great as your dominant aspirations.
> You will fall, rise or excel and move towards your dominant aspirations.

So often it will be your mental abilities coupled with your physical capacities that drive you to success. It may start with a thought that gives birth to a dream that spawns a desire, that triggers a passion. This passion will grow over time into commitment, and the commitment will become action leading to success.

Several years ago I was invited to a dinner party. I began meeting people I had never met before and finding out about their life stories. That's when I met Bill Irwin. Bill is totally blind. As I began to talk to Bill, I eventually got to the point were I said to him, "Bill tell me about your life? Tell me something that you have done even while you've been blind? That's when Bill disclosed to me his passion that led him to action. He told me that he had always wanted to hike the Appalachian Trail. It took time, and it took patience and practice. A lot of people tried to talk him out of it. They said it was too far and too dangerous. He could get lost or killed. But one day he and his dog Orient set out on the Appalachian Trail down in Georgia, and they hiked all the way to Maine, arriving eight months later. He is a man who understood the obstacle in front of him. He is a man who saw success even though he couldn't see the trail. He didn't let his lack of sight be transferred into a lack of vision.

Rose knew all too well that obstacles like age can get in the way of you living out your dreams. She pressed past that barrier and inspired so many others to do the same. Here is her story told through the eyes of one she influenced:

The first day of school our professor introduced himself and challenged us to get to know someone we didn't already know. I stood up to look around when a gentle hand touched my shoulder. I turned around to find a wrinkled, little old lady beaming up at me with a smile that lit up her entire being. She said, "Hi handsome! My name is Rose. I'm eighty-seven years old. Can I give you a hug?" I laughed and enthusiastically responded, "Of course you may!" and she gave me a giant squeeze.

"Why are you in college at such a young, innocent age?" I asked. She jokingly replied, "I'm here to meet a rich husband, get married, have a couple of children, and then retire and travel." "No, seriously," I asked. I was curious what may have motivated her to be taking on this challenge at her age. "I always dreamed of having a college education, and now I'm getting one!" she told me.

After class we walked to the student union building and shared a chocolate milkshake. We became instant friends. Everyday for the next three months we would leave class together and talk nonstop. I was mesmerized listening to the "time machine" as she shared her wisdom and experience with me.

Over the course of the year, Rose became a campus icon, and she easily made friends wherever she went. She loved to dress up, and she reveled in the attention bestowed upon her from the other students. She was living it up.

At the end of the semester we invited Rose to speak at our football banquet. I'll never forget what she taught us. She was introduced and stepped up to the podium. As she began to deliver her prepared speech, she dropped her three-by-five cards on the floor. Frustrated and a little embarrassed she leaned into the microphone and simply said, "I'm sorry I'm so jittery. I gave up beer for lent and this whiskey is killing me! I'll never get my speech back in order so let me just tell you what I know." As we laughed, she cleared her throat and continued. "We do not stop playing because we are old; we grow old because we stop playing. There are only four secrets to staying young, being happy and achieving success. You have to laugh and find humor every day. You've got to have a dream. When you lose your dreams, you die. We have so many people walking around who are dead and don't even know it.

"There is a huge difference between growing older and growing up. If you are nineteen years old and lie in bed for one full year and don't do one productive thing, you will turn twenty years old. If I am eighty-seven years old and stay in bed for a year and never do anything, I will turn eighty-eight. Anybody can grow older. That doesn't take any talent or ability. The idea is to grow up by always finding the opportunity in change.

"Have no regrets. The elderly usually don't have regrets for what we did, but rather for things we did not do. The only people who fear death are those with regrets." She concluded her speech by courageously singing "The Rose." She challenged each of us to study the lyrics and live them out in our daily lives.

At the year's end, Rose finished the college degree she had begun all those years ago. One week after graduation Rose died peacefully in her sleep. Over two thousand college students attended her funeral in tribute to the wonderful woman who taught by example that it's never too late to be all you can be. Remember that growing older is mandatory; growing up is optional.

What is stopping you? Is it your age? Are you struggling with physical difficulties? Is it your social standing? Is there a financial obstacle in your way? It's time you took advice from the woman that went back to school. Don't just grow old; grow up. Find some worthwhile obstacle in your life, and commit yourself to overcoming it. You'll never regret it.

NOTABLE QUOTABLE: "SUCCESS IS TO BE MEASURED NOT SO MUCH
BY THE POSITION THAT ONE HAS REACHED IN LIFE AS BY THE
OBSTACLES WHICH HE HAS OVERCOME WHILE TRYING TO SUCCEED."
BOOKER T. WASHINGTON

DIRECTIVE 4—
SURROUND YOURSELF WITH THE RIGHT PEOPLE

A young lady was complaining to her father about how tough life was getting for her. She complained about her lack of money, how difficult things were at school, about not having the transportation that she needed, not having the right friends, and not being in the popular circles. Without a word, her father took her to the kitchen and instructed her to sit down. Then he put a pot on the stove and set some water to boiling. A few minutes later he took some carrots and cut them up and dropped them into the pot. Then he took an egg and dropped the egg into the pot. Lastly he took some instant coffee and dropped the coffee into the pot. After each of these three ingredients had been boiling for a little while he strained them and set them out on the counter.

Then he said to his daughter, "There is something to be learned from the ingredients in the pot. The water was the same for all of them, but if you'll notice, the egg has been hardened from the hot water. You will also notice that the carrots have been softened by the same hot water. But see what the coffee did to the water. The coffee wasn't changed by the hot water. The coffee changed the hot water. The lesson is simple: your environment may have an impact on you. But if you do things right, you can have an impact on your environment." Be careful with what you surround yourself with. It's no secret - whatever your environment is, it will have an impact on you.

The people that you run with will either take you up or they will pull you down. There are very few neutral relationships. Your relationships will have an influence on you. If you have friends who are not taking you in a positive direction, then you need to reevaluate what a friend is. Good friends bring you up. Good friends make you a better person. Good friends care more about you than they do about the relationship they have with you. If your friends are not bringing you up, as harsh as this may sound, you need to change your friends.

There's a story told of a parrot that was on a farm and got loose from the farmer's house. He found himself on a wire amongst a bunch of crows. The crows were making a lot of noise and swooping down on the farmer while eating the grain he was trying to plant. In an effort to rid the farm of these pests, the farmer got his shotgun out and blasted that flock of crows. He killed most of the crows and badly wounded the parrot. The parrot flew and limped his way back home, returning to his cage. The children saw that the ruffled parrot was in a bad way. They asked what happened to the parrot and the parrot called out, "Bad company, bad company."

I can clearly say that almost all the problems that I had growing up were related to the guys I ran with. I am not excusing my behavior, but I know that most of the time it was because of the people that I was around. The driving force that propels you to the people you are around comes from a deep desire that all of us have. We all have an innate desire to belong. We desperately want to be accepted, to be included in a group. Because of that so often we will compromise our principles and ideals just so that we can have somebody say, "I like you, I accept you, I want you to be with me." This can easily lead us to join the wrong circles. The Chinese have a saying that applies here: "If one lies down with dogs, he wakes up with fleas."

Several years ago, I found myself touring in and around Russia. One thing we were told very directly by the people in charge of our tour was that under no circumstances were we to eat uncooked vegetables or drink the water. So as I visited the country, whenever I got thirsty I would have a soft drink. I spent twenty three days in Russia, and at the end of those twenty three days I may have consumed over seventy soft drinks. One day I looked in the mirror and realized my teeth were brown. They weren't brown because I didn't brush them. They were brown because they were constantly exposed to cola. The cola was affecting the shade of my teeth. Needless to say, I was concerned. I stayed away from the cola when I got home and I brushed my teeth more often than I ever did before, and the stains faded. The point is, my teeth turned the color of what they were exposed to.

As was mentioned before, Roger Bannister was the first man to run the sub four-minute mile. What most people don't know is that he didn't accomplish this feat alone. He had what is known as rabbits to run with him. Chris Chataway and Chris Brasher were the rabbits. Their job was to go out hard and go out fast. They knew they couldn't keep up the pace and run a sub four-minute mile. Their purpose was to pull Roger along and give him the proper pace to put him in the best position to break the sub four-minute mile. Roger Bannister was successful because of who he ran with. These were men who were interested in his success. Peers can be positive or negative. The key is to surround oneself with the right people all the time.

When dealing with the different types of people to be surrounded by, the analogy of a boxer is very important. I started watching boxing when I was very young. Although I didn't know much about the practical side of boxing, I knew there were two fighters in the center of the ring, but there were a lot more people involved in what was needed to put these men in the ring. At the very least, there are four people a boxer needs to have to make him successful. Likewise they are the same type of people we need to build into our lives to be successful. One person is a promoter; this is a person who tells everybody how great their boxer is. They brag on that person. They're a cheerleader for their person. They give good advice to the boxer. A promoter in our lives will do the very same thing. He will cheer us on. He will promote us. He will speak well of us, and he will give us advice. He has our best interests at heart.

Another person the boxer needs in his life is a trainer. A trainer is the person that has been where the boxer is and is where he wants to go. They understand life. They understand what it takes to win. They understand what the fighter has to do in order to be in the absolute best shape to withstand all the things that will come his way in the ring. Likewise, we need somebody who is a trainer for us. This is a person who can be called a mentor. To help us succeed, they can share with us their wisdom and experience.

The boxer also needs a sparing partner in the ring. A sparing partner's job is to hurt the fighter a little so he doesn't get hurt a lot. They are there to help him anticipate all the problems he will encounter in the ring. Likewise, in life, we need a sparing partner. This is called an accountability person. He is someone who will show us our "blind spots," thereby hurting us a little in order to prevent us from getting hurt a lot in life.

Then there is the cut man. He is the person who helps put the boxer back together again, so he can return to the ring and fight. He takes care of all the cuts on the boxer's face and the bruises on his body. In the ring in life we will experience cuts, and we will experience injuries and we will need somebody who will come alongside us and patch up the broken places, putting us back together again, so we can go back into the ring of life and fight our best.

Beyond people, it's also your environment and your thoughts that influence your life. Your first and last thought of the day often sets you up for success or defeat. What your workspace and your study space look like has a lot to do with how you perform. Your environment puts you in a position to be successful or sets you up to fail. Because you become what you surround yourself with, it is imperative that you expose yourself to people and things that make you think and make you laugh, things that energize you and make you everything you need to be.

NOTABLE QUOTABLE: "A BURDEN HELD IS A BURDEN MULTIPLIED. A BURDEN SHARED IS A BURDEN DIVIDED." STEVEN A. JIRGAL

Directive 5—
Stop Acting Like Life Is Always Supposed To Be Fair

Tom and Nancy were ready to realize a dream come true. Tom had just retired from his firm. They had plenty of money. They began to build their dream home, a home in which they could be comfortable and live out their days together. The house was completed, and Tom and Nancy prepared to move in. That's when Tom's world came crashing down. Nancy shared with him that she no longer loved him and had fallen in love with a man name Stan, who "happened to be" the builder of their home. She was leaving Tom, and she was moving in with Stan. Needless to say, Tom was devastated. He moved into their dream home by himself, and Nancy moved in with Stan. Five days after Nancy left Tom, Stan suffered a massive heart attack and died. Nancy was left with nothing, no home, no money, and no place to go.

There is something inside of us that in a small way wants to cheer at the result of what happened. A woman betrayed her husband, committed adultery, and was left devastated herself. That's the way we want life to work out. But in reality it rarely turns out that way.

The truth is bad things happen to good people and bad things happen to bad people. It is also true that good things happen to good people and good things happen to bad people. Because you don't consider yourself a bad person doesn't shield you from cancer, heartache, or even gravity. If you understand this, it helps you when life's struggles come. Life is made of people, and people are fallible. You can't build a perfect machine from damaged parts. Sooner or later your rose colored glasses will be broken. When that happens and you don't have the proper perspective, you may become cynical and bitter about life. Life is not about being dealt a good hand. So often life is about learning to play a poor hand well. The old saying is true: life is not about waiting for the clouds to pass; it's about learning how to dance in the rain.

Not long ago the news coverage was filled with a man named Bernard Madoff. He was the chairman of the NASDAQ stock exchange and was involved in a scheme that robbed people of billions of dollars. These were good people. These were people who had trusted him, and they gave their entire life savings to this man to be invested so they could retire comfortably. In the end it was found that he lied and cheated them out of every cent they had, and now they were left with nothing. He went to jail, and they were forced to go back to work. It's just not fair! Yet deep inside each of us is a desire that we have that life should be fair. We not only want things to be fair, but we also want them to be fair according to our own terms. We want the person who cut us off in traffic to be pulled over by a police officer or have a wreck. We want a cheater to get diseases, and we wish heartaches upon the one who talks bad about us. But without doubt, that is not how life always goes. Life can be devastating sometimes. But success in life is found not so much in what happens to us but our reactions to what happens to us.

Recently in our community we buried a little four year old boy with a heart condition named Timmy. There was nothing bad in his life. He didn't live long enough to develop a lifestyle that would cause him to deserve what happened to him. Without question his mom and dad were heartbroken. We don't understand why this happened. It is not fair, but we've got to put the pieces together, and we've got to march on through life. The fact is that life in general can bring great difficulties. No one is immune. People will cheat you. People will take advantage of you. People will disappoint you and slander you and leave you. No one is absolved from the issues of life that are difficult to handle. If we understand that, we won't be blindsided and immobilized when something bad does happen to those of us who consider ourselves to be good people.

DIRECTIVE 6 —
LIVE YOUR LIFE AS A MARATHON, NOT A SPRINT

There once was a fellow who, with his dad, farmed a little piece of land. Several times a year they would load up the old ox-drawn cart with vegetables and go into the nearest city to sell their produce. Except for their name and the patch of ground, father and son had little in common. The old man believed in taking it easy. The boy was usually in a hurry, the go-getter type.

One morning, bright and early, they hitched up the ox to the loaded cart and started on the long journey. The son figured that if they walked faster, kept going all day and night, they'd make market by early the next morning. So he kept prodding the ox with a stick, urging the beast to get a move on.

"Take it easy, son," said the old man. "You'll last longer."

"But if we get to the market ahead of the others, we'll have a better chance of getting good prices," argued the son.

No reply. Dad just pulled his hat down over his eyes and fell asleep on the seat. Itchy and irritated, the young man kept goading the ox to walk faster. His stubborn pace refused the change.

Four hours and four miles down the road, they came to a little house. The father woke up, smiled and said, "Here's your uncle's place. Let's stop in and say hello."

"But we've lost an hour already," complained the hotshot.

"Then a few minutes won't matter. My brother and I live so close, yet we see each other so seldom," the father answered slowly.

The boy fidgeted and fumed while the two old men laughed and talked away almost an hour. On the move again, the man took his turn leading the ox. As they approached a fork in the road, the father led the

25

ox to the right.

"The left is the shorter way," said the son.

"I know it," replied the old man, "but this way is so much prettier."

"Have you no respect for time?" the young man asked impatiently.

"Oh, I respect it very much! That's why I like to look at beauty and enjoy each moment to the fullest."

The winding path led through graceful meadows, wildflowers, and along a rippling stream all of which the young man missed as he churned within, preoccupied and boiling with anxiety. He didn't even notice how lovely the sunset was that day.

Twilight found them in what looked like a huge, colorful garden. The old man breathed in the aroma, listened to the bubbling brook, and pulled the ox to a halt. "Let's sleep here," he sighed.

"This is the last trip I'm taking with you, snapped his son. "You're more interested in watching sunsets and smelling flowers than in making money!"

"Why, that's the nicest thing you've said in a long time," smiled the dad. A couple of minutes later he was snoring as his boy glared back at the stars. The night dragged by slowly; the son was restless.

Before sunrise the young man hurriedly shook his father awake. They hitched up and went on. About a mile down the road they happened upon another farmer who was a total stranger trying to pull his cart out of a ditch.

"Let's give him a hand," whispered the old man.

"And lose more time?" the boy exploded.

"Relax son, you might be in a ditch sometime yourself. We need to help others in need. Don't forget that." The boy looked away in anger.

It was almost eight o'clock that morning by the time the other cart was back on the road. Suddenly, a great flash split the sky. What sounded like thunder followed. Beyond the hills, the sky grew dark.

"Looks like rain in the big city," said the old man.

"If we had hurried, we'd be almost sold out by now," grumbled his son.

"Take it easy, you'll last longer. And you'll enjoy life so much more," counseled the kind old gentleman.

It was late in the afternoon by the time they got to the hill over-looking the city. They stopped and stared down at it for a long, long time. Neither of them said a word. Finally, the young man put his hand on his father's shoulder and said," I see what you mean, Dad."

They turned their cart around and began to roll slowly away from what had once been the city of Hiroshima.

Friends, it is important to stop and smell the roses. Peter Marshall said, "We are in such a hurry that we hate to miss one panel of a revolving door."

Years ago some of the most blessed times families enjoyed was time spent on the front porch. So many front porches are gone in America. That was the place where people would go to sit and enjoy lemonade, homemade ice cream, stories, and songs. Neighbors would go for a walk and never get far because they would always stop to sit on the front steps or porch of a neighbor down the street, enjoying their company. Somehow we decided that life is supposed to be hurried through and our desires have been turned upside down so that we work at our play and play at our work. We miss so much in terms of relationships. An unknown writer said, "The mark of a successful man is one who has spent the entire day on the bank of a river without feeling guilty about it." Life is meant to be enjoyed, but when the pace of life is too fast for us to notice the people and things around us, then the enjoyment of life fades. The sun is quickly setting on the day of the hand written note. We'd rather fax or text somebody, shoot an e-mail, or even leave a message on a machine. We are missing so much when we don't experience those face to face and voice to voice encounters with the people around us. Someone has said I value my friends who make time on their calendar for me. But I cherish my friends who don't consult their calendar.

The key is to be deliberate and intentional about life. We shouldn't miss the blessings that are waiting for us:

-the giggle of a child
-the warmth of a fire
-the mystery of the stars
-the innocence of a baby
-the enthusiasm of a young person

-the wonder of a flower
-the beauty of a sunset
-the value of a good book
-the love of a life mate
-the firmness of a handshake
-the glory of a sunny day
-the power of the rain
-the warmth of the sun
-the freshness of undisturbed snow.

My mother understood this, and she placed a lot of value in the relationships that she developed around her. For years she had a typed laminate attached to her keys. It simply said, "Slow me down, Lord." Years later I came across the rest of that poem. It's by Wilferd Arlan Peterson who penned:"*Slow me down Lord. Ease the pounding of my heart by the quieting of my mind. Steady my hurried pace. Give me, amidst the day's confusion, the calmness of the everlasting hills. Break the tensions of my nerves and muscles with the soothing music of singing streams that live in my memory.*

Help me to know the magical, restoring power of sleep. Teach me the art of taking 'minute vacations' slowing down to look at a flower, to chat with a friend, to read a few lines from a good book. Remind me of the fable of the hare and the tortoise: that the race is not always to the swift: that there is more to life than measuring its speed. Let me look up at the branches of the towering oak and know that it grew slowly and well. Inspire me to send my own roots down deep into the soil of life's endearing values...that I may grow toward the stars of my greater destiny."

At the ending of the day you and I need to be able to say that we have lived this day well. It's important for us to reflect on something that we can laugh at, someone that we have helped, something that we have thought deeply about, something we plan to engage in, or something worthwhile that was done. Because life is a marathon, it's important that we pace ourselves and take breaks, rest, enjoy those around us and finish well.

NOTABLE QUOTABLE, "THE BOW WILL BREAK IF IT IS ALWAYS BENT" (GREEK PHILOSOPHY)

DIRECTIVE 7—
LEARN FROM MISTAKES

Generally you will find that you meet three people in your life. The first type of person is a fool. A fool is somebody that never learns. A bumper sticker says, "A fool and his money are soon partying." The fools that you come across in life are not hard to find. It takes very little effort to spot them. It's the person who is always broke. He doesn't want a hand up; he wants a hand out, and you constantly have to rescue him. He is broke, bruised, bellyaching, blaming, and sticks out from the crowd like a sore thumb. A friend of mine works in the poultry industry, and he recently described a man who works for him who is a fool. This man doesn't know how to handle money. He can't keep a dollar in his pocket, and he is always in trouble. When he gets paid on Friday, he has no money a week later. Along with not knowing how to handle money, he doesn't know how to handle himself, and he is continuously making the same mistakes.

Another type of person you meet is a smart person. This is a person who makes mistakes and admits he makes mistakes, and then he learns from his mistakes. You probably have scars on different places of your body. They are the telltale signs of a mistake. But you'll notice that on your body you probably don't have two scars in the same place brought about the same way. Why is that? It's simply because you have learned from your mistakes.

Not long ago my daughter decided she wanted to have a turtle as a pet. Since we live out in the country, I wasn't about to go to a pet store and pay money so she could have her pet turtle. I decided that it would be a great adventure for my daughter and me to go out and catch our own. We tried several times, but the turtles were always too fast and too alert to be caught. Finally we found a pond in the woods that very few people knew about. We hiked through the woods out to this pond where we came upon the perfect turtle, a painted turtle a little bit smaller than my fist. As we approached it, I had visions of where we were going to put this turtle and what we were going to name him. The turtle was sound asleep. I got closer and closer until I was about four feet from him. Suddenly, he opened his eyes and scurried into the water. The entire pond was covered with a blanket of green duckweed. I reasoned that perhaps the turtle would think that because it couldn't see us, we couldn't see him, and he might be right there by the edge of the shore on the bottom of the pond. So I knelt down and reached into the water to catch this little fellow. I felt around, and a soon as I reached the bottom of the pond, WHAM! A large snapping turtle latched on to my forearm. I immediately yanked my hand out of the water, and the snapper flopped onto the land and then it scampered back into the water. I was cut, and bleeding and my daughter was in a panic. But if I live 150 more years, I will never forget the fact that I did something foolish. I am smart enough to know that I will never put myself in this position again.

Now if you remember that story, and it causes you to act in a certain way that protects you, then you fall into the best category of all. It is the wise category. A fool never learns from his mistakes, and a smart person learns from the mistakes he makes. But the truly wise person pays attention, remembers and learns from the mistakes of other people. He reads the signs, makes mental notes and heeds the warnings. He is the person who wears eye protection in the shop, fastens his seat belt, and obeys signs that say stay away from the edge. And because he learns from other's mistakes, he avoids trouble in his life.

Following is an autobiography in five short paragraphs and it clearly depicts various responses to an identical problem. It's very easy to see where the person is a fool, smart, and wise.

1. I walk down the street. There is a deep hole in the sidewalk. I fall in. I am lost. I am helpless. It isn't my fault. It takes forever to find a way out.

2. I walk down the street. There is a deep hole in the

sidewalk. I pretend I don't see it. I fall in. I can't believe I'm in the same place, but it isn't my fault. It still
takes a long time to get out.

3. I walk down the street. There is a deep hole in the
sidewalk. I see it is there. I still fall in. It's a habit. My
eyes are open. I know where I am. It is my fault. I get
out immediately.

4. I walk down the street. There is a deep hole in the sidewalk. I walk around it.

5. I walk down a different street. (Portia Nelson-Tales
from the Heart)

The mistakes you make today could be the landing,
the learning, or the launching point to your life. The choice is
yours.

NOTABLE QUOTABLE: "THOSE WHO FAIL TO LEARN FROM HISTORY
ARE DOOMED TO REPEAT IT." WINSTON CHURCHILL

DIRECTIVE 8—
KNOWLEDGE IS POWER - GET ALL YOU CAN

A young lady in college who was in the middle of her final exams for the fall semester. In a particular class she failed to study properly and quickly realized she was completely unprepared for the questions staring at her from her desk. The test was loaded with essay questions, and she had no idea how to answer any of them. So she worked her way through it as best she could and then wrote on the top of her paper, "God alone knows the answers to these questions - Merry Christmas." When she returned after the Christmas break, she got her test grade back in the mailbox and at the top of her test grade the professor had written, "God gets an 'A', and you get an 'F.' Happy New Year."

The point is that the young lady did not have the power to get a good grade because she didn't have the knowledge she needed, and beside that, she didn't have the knowledge when she needed it. The adage is it's not what you know but who you know. But it goes even farther than that. In fact it's not what you know, and it's not who you know, it's when you know it that makes the difference in your life. Everyone knows that it is possible for the Titanic to sink. But no one needs to know that now. They needed to know that on April 14, 1912, the night the massive ship struck the iceberg. So it truly is when you know it that makes the big difference.

A pilot who sits in front of an instrument panel in his cockpit only has half of what he needs. He has the instruments, but what he's got to be able to do is read them at the proper moment. Generally, you gain knowledge in your life through three different venues. People: Knowledge will be gleaned by your exposure to people (good or bad). Obviously if you want to gain the knowledge you need from people, you must be willing to be around people. You have to admit you don't know everything, and you have to come willing to learn.

Years ago, I found myself in Alaska at an anniversary celebration. I was working the room asking people where they came from, what they did for a living, where they live, and generally learning about their life experiences. I went up to an elderly gentleman and asked him his name. I asked him where he was from, and then I asked him to tell me something that he felt was significant about his life. He related to me a wonderful story of being in the Air Force and being stationed in Honolulu, Hawaii. He was there the day the Japanese bombed Pearl Harbor. I found out that they had decimated our ships and our airfields and our planes. There were only two planes that got off the ground to counter the attack of the Japanese. The man I was talking to was in one of them. What an encounter, what a story!

Information: Another area that you gain knowledge from is information itself. Information will either be true or false. One of the best places to gain information is from books. Very few people have the desire to read today. There is so much to be gained from an experience with a book. In my life I have read hundreds of books, and I am in a position to talk on lots of different subjects because of the knowledge I've gained from time with the written word. The problem with only gaining your information from other people is that you're forced to take their viewpoint on particular subjects. But when you read a book, you can use your imagination, and you can develop creativity through the natural thinking process.

Experiences: Another area you can gain knowledge from is experiences. The experiences in your life can be either positive or negative. These experiences may enable you up to fix the problems in your life or to facilitate success in your life.

Many people are familiar with the life of Jackie Robinson, the first black man to play professional baseball. He lived in a day when prejudge reined and there was great animosity between the races. Black people were discriminated against and were not allowed to play professional baseball. But Jackie Robinson had such a gift of the game that he broke through the barrier of race and played for the Brooklyn Dodgers. The crowds did not agree with Commissioner Branch Ricky that blacks should be allowed to play so when he was first introduced, he was booed. The game could not start because there was so much debris on the playing field. But then something happened. An experience occurred that changed the game and Jackie Robinson forever. Right in the middle of all the mayhem and booing by the fans, Harold Henry "Pee Wee" Reese walked from short stop over to second base and put his arm around Jackie Robinson. It was a message that all the fans saw. The message was he is a Brooklyn Dodger. He is with me, and you need to cheer for him. Then the crowd settled down, the game began, and baseball has never been the same. Years later, Jackie Robinson said, "That arm around my shoulder saved my career." The experience of a white man's arm over a black man's shoulder gave the fans the knowledge that this man was a Brooklyn Dodger, this man could play baseball, and this man was worthy of respect.

It's very important that you avail yourself of new experiences. In new experiences comes knowledge and with new experiences comes power.

Allow me to share with you the nine rules of academic success I share with college students whenever I get a chance to talk with them about their academic career.

1. Treat college as a job. Plan on spending at least eight hours each day on this academic job.
2. Go to class and be on time.
3. Sit up front. It helps you pay attention, limits distractions, and makes you accountable. It's hard to hide on the front row.
4. Engage your professor respectfully. It demonstrates that you're prepared and mentally involved.
5. Take notes. "A dull pencil remembers more than a sharp mind."
6. Dress for success. This shows your instructor that you are respectful and serious.

7. Do your own work. Earn your own grades. Pride and shame can both last a lifetime.
8. Don't procrastinate. Keeping up is easier than catching up.
9. Study in a secluded place. Find your spot away from obvious distractions and determine to do nothing there but work.

Knowledge is power. Not only does knowledge give you power to help yourself, it gives you power to help others. Years ago a scientist named Louis Pasteur had the opportunity to help so many others because of his scientific discoveries. While walking on a farm with a friend, they were discussing what needed to be done about a particular disease that was ravishing all of France. As they walked along, Pasteur noticed that there was an area of the pasture where the grass was brown. It wasn't growing, and he asked his friend about it. He was informed that this was the area where they buried the cows from last season that died of this disease. Louis Pasteur, because he understood something about the disease realized at that point that the disease could easily be transmitted from an animal into the grass and into the cows that ate that grass. Because of the power he gained through that knowledge he was in a position to help other people and stop the disease.

People who have knowledge have options. They can do something with the knowledge and better their life and the lives of others. But there are pitfalls that are attached to knowledge. The wrong knowledge or the right knowledge at the wrong time will equal failure. But the right knowledge at the right time will lead to success.

It all comes down to people. It's people from whom we grow. It's whom we laugh with, play with, cry with, and who we spend time with that makes a difference in our lives. You will never receive a call from your possessions. They will never tell you that they love you. If there is any joy that comes from spending time with your things, you can be sure that it is only temporary joy.

People are consistently looking to solve their problems by

surrounding themselves by things. But the solutions to so many problems we have in life are found in surrounding ourselves with people. The fact is, we are wired to be inter-related. We are social beings. Fulfillment is really found in being around people. We are symbiotic creatures in our relationship to other people. Truly fulfilling relationships involve the idea that "I need you, and I need to be needed by you." When either of those things is not present in a relationship, the relationship is not going be all it can be. A true friend is somebody who you need, but it is also somebody that you can pour your life into. Generally you can only manage seven deep and solid relationships at any given time in your life. The others will be acquaintances and friends, but for the deep lasting and stable relationships that you want in your life, you will only have about seven of these at one particular time. The key is to identify those seven and pour your life into them.

Another aspect of the people in your life is that you must establish yourself as a friend. By that I mean you must be friend-worthy. There are people who don't have many friends. Some people don't have any close friends, and often times it's simply because they are not friend-worthy. In order to be friend-worthy you must be willing to spend time, energy, and perhaps some money. Lots of times you need to be an ear more than a tongue. You must develop a history with that other person. The truth is that loving things and using people leads to emptiness. But using things and loving people leads to fulfillment. When you surround yourself with people, you open yourself up to information and experience, and therein lies the secret of gaining knowledge.

NOTABLE QUOTABLE: "A CURIOUS PERSON WHO ASKS QUESTIONS MAY BE A FOOL FOR FIVE MINUTES; HE WHO NEVER ASKS QUESTIONS REMAINS A FOOL FOREVER." VERN MCLELLAN

DIRECTIVE 9 —
UNDERSTAND THAT PERSONAL FREEDOM COMES FROM PERSONAL DISCIPLINE

This idea runs counter to what the world's message is. The world says that freedom consists of doing whatever I want, wherever I want, however I want, and with whomever I want. But when you ask an alcoholic, a drug addict, and a prisoner if they feel free, invariable they will say no. What caused them to be the alcoholic or the drug addict or the prisoner is the idea that they can do anything they want. They believed they could ingest anything they want or could do anything they want with their freedom but in the end they wind up a prisoner of a disease, a substance, or the judicial system.

Coaches and athletes understand that discipline in practice causes you to react automatically when you go over the same action repeatedly. You're disciplining your body to do automatically what it has to do in a given situation. We must learn that what you do when you don't have to will determine what you will be when you can't help it.

When I was in college, I always had the discipline to get an early start on all my papers. I made a habit of choosing a particular paper that I was going to work on first, and the Friday after it was assigned, I would go to the library and gather up all the books that I could. I wanted to be the first one to get the books so they wouldn't be picked over by the other students who had the same assignment. I gathered all the information I thought I needed to write the paper, and then the following Saturday morning I would hunker down in one of the classrooms in the basement of an educational building. In short order, I would outline my paper and begin writing. With two undergraduate degrees, three master degrees, and my doctorate, I only asked for an extension one time. I never handed in a paper late. That freed me emotionally from the panic of the end of the semester. It freed me from the deadlines and commitments that come naturally in individual classes. Often times, at the end of the semester I was free to do all the social things I wanted, because I chose to be disciplined at the beginning, while so many other students who delayed and procrastinated were struggling over deadlines, prisoners of a time clock.

The person who goes to work and earns enough money enjoys a vacation. An individual who exercises and diets becomes fit and enjoys a better physical quality of life. The man or woman who drives the speed limit is free from the worry of being caught by the police and fined for speeding.

Discipline is ignited by priorities. What do you really want? What do you really need? What price are you willing to pay to get those? "When your want to becomes your have to, then your maybe becomes your probably."

We must remember that kites fly because there is a string. If there is no string, then the kite falls. The thing that ties the kite to the earth allows it to fly. False freedom says do as you want. But true freedom says do as you ought.

NOTABLE QUOTABLE: "WE DO WHAT WE HAVE TO SO WE CAN DO WHAT WE WANT TO." MOVIE: THE GREAT DEBATERS.

DIRECTIVE 10 —
CHOOSE YOUR BATTLES - YOU DON'T HAVE TO ATTEND EVERY FIGHT YOU ARE INVITED TO

Some very harsh and untrue criticism was leveled at a local judge. He was walking with his friend one day when his friend brought up the subject of this critic and said to the judge, "Are you never going to address the unfair issues that he is bringing up about you?" The judge said, "You know when I go outside my house at night and I look up and there is a full moon, so often I hear dogs barking at the moon, but I have noticed that the moon never barks back. It just keeps on shining. That is the position I've chosen to take."

You and I must make a decision about what hills are worth fighting on and what hills are worth dying on. We must prioritize our lives and the issues that are before us. Abraham Lincoln, president during one of the most tumultuous times of our nation, understood this. He said, "If I tried to read, much less answer, all the criticisms made of me and all the attacks leveled against me, this office would have to be closed for all other business. I do the best I know how, the very best I can. And I mean to keep on doing this, down to the very end. If the end brings me out all wrong, ten angels swearing I had been right would make no difference. If the end brings me out all right, then what is said against me now will not amount to anything."

Critics are easy to find and easier to get bogged down by. When you've got a job to do, you cannot allow yourself to get sidetracked by those who are simply speaking loudly. Someone once said, "If you throw a stick at every barking dog, you will never make it to town."

41

Some questions need to be asked regarding whether or not an issue is worth addressing.

- Is it worth the emotional scar?
- Is it worth the loss of a relationship?
- Is it worth losing time?
- What will a victory or defeat cost me?
- What is the bottom line of the issue?
- In order to win will someone have to lose?
- Is it really any of my business?

Generally you can quickly see that some issues can become emotional. Religion and politics are truly emotional issues over which people can get heated very quickly. I learned a long time ago that if people wear their opinions on their hat or on their shirt, they wear it in their heart, and they will not be easily changed from their opinion. Most times I just avoid these encounters. When you hear of someone's opinion or you see their opinion you are seeing the What. The key to avoiding confrontation is to ask yourself, so what? Rule #1. Don't sweat the small stuff. Rule #2. It's all small stuff, and if you can't fight, flee and if you can't flee, flow.

You will avoid lots of scars that can come about from a confrontation. The person who rests best at night is the one who is at peace with God, with himself, and with others.

NOTABLE QUOTABLE: *"ANY DOG CAN OUT FIGHT A SKUNK BUT IT'S NOT WORTH IT."* ANONYMOUS

DIRECTIVE 11—
DEVELOP A CLEAR DEFINITION OF WINNING

As I've looked back on what it was like growing up and I deal with the concept of winning, I've found that the definition changed as I grew older. As a young boy, winning consisted of competition against obstacles and competition against people. I found that generally those who won were those who were the biggest, the fastest, and the strongest. As I moved through high school and college, winning was defined as conquering both people and things. For many in college it involved sexual encounters with the girls conquering the boys and the boys conquering the girls. Then moving into a business setting it became centered around conquest. Conquest for the business deals, conquest for money and things, and conquest of titles.

Basically, throughout the years winning amounted to comparison. It consisted of those who rose to the top in a situation and those who slipped to the bottom, those whose times where faster than others and those whose accomplishments outdistanced others. Comparison is a poor measure of winning because it always gives us the opportunity to be labeled what we're not. It's possible to outscore somebody and still not feel like you've won because you didn't do your best. It's also possible to work as hard as you can, giving everything you have, and come out on the short end but still feel victorious. So winning in some respects is a feeling, and if a comparison is to be made, it must be made in regard to ourselves.

An ageless anonymous writing sums up this concept well:

The Man in the Glass
When you get what you want in your struggles for self

And the world makes you king for a day,
Just go to the mirror and look at yourself
And see what that man has to say.
For it isn't your father or mother or wife
Whose judgment upon you must pass.
The fellow whose verdict counts most in your life
Is the one staring back from the glass.
You may be like Jack Horner and chisel a plum
And think you're a wonderful guy.
But the man in the glass says you're only a bum
If you can't look him straight in the eye.
He's the fellow to please-never mind all the rest,
For he's with you clear to the end.
And you've passed your most dangerous,
difficult test If the man in the glass is your friend.
You may fool the whole world down the pathway of years
And get pats on the back as you pass.
But your final reward will be heartache and tears
If you've cheated the man in the glass.

In our family we've come up with a clear definition of winning. We've had to share with our children what we expect from them in terms of success. When we did that, we overlaid these principles on their lives and covered areas such as athletics, performing arts, school, and even board games. One of the rules we shared with our children is this: winning consists of doing your best, and only you can determine this.

When I was a football player in high school, we had to run wind sprints. We learned very early that you can run at eighty percent and grimace at 100 percent. The goal was not to work as hard but to get the coaches to believe that you were giving an all out effort. But the only person who can determine whether or not you're doing your best is you. At the end of the day if you can honesty say, "I have lived this day to the fullest and I have done my absolute best," then there is no need of comparison to someone else. You can rest well in knowing that you have done the absolute best you could. We've also defined winning in our family as playing by the rules. It's not just when a referee, a policeman, or a teacher is watching, but deep down in your heart that you know that you did what's right and obeyed the rules. Knowing what you did was right empowers you to move forward in your life.

We've further defined a winner as someone who did not quit. The scoreboard doesn't count. It's what's in your heart in the effort you gave that really matters. When things get tough, there is a universal temptation to quit. There has never been a man or women, boy or girl, who has not been tempted to quit at something. Understanding that you will face the option of quitting and not giving in to that temptation gives you great confidence.

When our children were very young and they played soccer, I noticed that none of our children were on a team that outscored the other team. I know that some people brag about their teams being undefeated. Our children were always on the defeated side. In fact, there were a couple of seasons when they never won a game. But I always asked them three questions after every game was over; "Did you do your best? Did you play by the rules? Did you quit?" When my children said, "Yes, I did my best; yes, I played by the rules," and "no, I didn't quit," I always scooped them up in my arms, and I said, "Today you won!"

Stephen R. Covey relates a great story of how he learned the true meaning of winning:

> I was the junior varsity quarterback at the college I attended. The previous week, we had a great game. I threw for about five hundred yards, four or five touchdowns, and the newspaper started heralding me as the next great quarterback.
>
> The following week we got set to play one of the best teams in the nation. Their leading defensive lineman was a 275-pound quarterback-wrecking machine. We were playing at home for this big game. Of course, I wanted to play well in front of the home crowd. And my dad flew back from somewhere just to watch me play. I didn't think he would make it, but there he was just before the whistle blew.

I had the worst game of my life. The monster defensive lineman was all over me. He spent more time in our backfield than I did. My head was slammed into the ground so many times I was leaving divots. I swear I wasn't on my feet after the snap for longer than three seconds. Of course, I didn't throw one touchdown. I did, however, rack up an impressive number of interceptions. We lost by about thirty points.

During the game I must have looked pathetic. After the game I was embarrassed. Nobody would talk to me. You know how it goes when you play terribly? In the locker room, everybody avoids you. So I showered and dressed in silence. When I came out of the locker room, my dad was waiting for me. He took me in his arms, hugged me, looked me right in the eyes and said, "That's the best game I have ever seen you play. Not because you won or threw the most touchdowns. But because I have never seen you be as tough as you had to be out there today. You were getting beat. Yet you kept getting up. I have never been so proud of you."

We must not let the world force us to live according to its definition of winning. We have got to come to our own conclusions regarding winning and losing and be courageous enough to stand by them.

NOTABLE QUOTABLE: "FAME IS A VAPOR, POPULARITY AN ACCIDENT, RICHES TAKE WING, AND ONLY CHARACTER ENDURES."
HORACE GREELEY

DIRECTIVE *12*—
LIVE *A* BALANCED LIFE

So often our lives are lived in extremes. We wind up with conflicted pursuits. We work at our play and we play at our work and we rest at our service. All this leads to a life that is out of balance. The person who only studies and never gets involved socially is labeled a cave salamander. The person who only lives to play develops a lifestyle of laziness. The workaholic who is only interested in the next dollar or the next deal is not fit to be in many social circles because of truncated social skills.

If you are going to live a balanced life and be in a position to move forward, then let me propose to you five areas you need to keep in balance.

1. *Work.* Some have said, "If you've got eight hours to kill, you might as well work it to death," or "nobody ever drowned in sweat." But if work is all you do, it will wear you down and shorten your life. The key is to work to live and not live to work. It is said that "all work and no play makes Jack a dull boy," but all work and no play also makes Jack a candidate for an early grave.

2. *Play.* When you build play into your life, you relieve the tensions of life and the problems that overstress can bring. Science has demonstrated tremendous benefits of laughter and how healthy it can be. The Bible says, "Laughter does the heart good like a medicine" (Proverbs 17:22). We've discovered so many of the beneficial affects of hardy laughter. It's important that we build play and stress relievers into our lives.

It's also important that we get with friends with whom we develop adventures and build memories. My wife and I are involved in something we call "the Friday club." Periodically we get together with two other couples and spend time eating, socializing, and going on adventures together. We've been to museums, to outdoor centers and have gone hiking together. It's all part of a plan we have built into our lives.

3. *Study.* Study is an area that we somehow have decided ends with the completion of a high school, college, or advanced degree. A friend of mine was interviewing for a job, and as he shared with those interviewing him, he said, "And I completed my studies at the university." When he got done, one of the interviewers pulled him aside and said, "Sir, can I propose to you that you never stop learning? Never complete your learning with a particular age or particular institution. Always learn."

I've adopted that idea in my own life. I've taken classes outside of a degree program, and I have surrounded myself with things from which I can continually learn. One of my goals for many years has been to read 24 books a year. I will challenge you to learn to study. Continue to study and grow from your studies. Write things down. Ask questions. Commit to being well versed on a particular topic. You will find that study can be a way of growing and advancing like you never understood it before.

4. *Serve.* Albert Schweitzer said, "I don't know what your destiny will be, but one thing I know, the only ones among you who will be really happy are the ones who have sought and found how to serve."

If you look on a map of the Middle East, you will come to a unique area of Israel. In that area of Israel you will find a dominating river called the Jordan River. At the head of the Jordan River is the Sea of Galilee. The Sea of Galilee is lush, green, and teeming with life. It is a tourist attraction, and it's where many businesses thrive. There are immeasurable amounts of activity going on at the Sea of Galilee. The Jordan River flows from the Sea of Galilee and moves down to the lowest body of water in the world, the Dead Sea. It is called the Dead Sea because it has no life in it whatsoever. The salinity of the Dead Sea is so high even bacteria will not grow in it. There is absolutely nothing alive in the Dead Sea. The reason why the Dead Sea is dead is because it only has a receiving port. There is no out port like the Sea of

Galilee so it takes water in and the cycle of receiving water and evaporation takes place. This increase in the concentration of minerals makes it impossible for any life to exist.

That's how it is in our lives. In order for us to have life, to thrive and to grow, and to be everything we can be, we have to have an area in our lives where we take in but also an area in our lives were we give out in service to others. In this world there are givers and there are takers. The takers eat well, but you will find that the givers sleep will. You must intentionally build into your life an area where you can serve in your school, your work, your community, or your church and make it a continual place of giving.

5. *Rest.* Very few people address the idea of rest. We are all involved in it, but perhaps not in the proper amount. John, a seasoned businessman, was in a job interview. As he was negotiating the benefits portion of the job, he was informed that his former time of service would not count toward time off for vacation. In his previous job he had one month off each year. He let them know that he can do more work in eleven months than he could in twelve months. They saw his viewpoint and gave him the desired four weeks off.

A story is told of a man who was going on safari. Because of business needs that had to be addressed, he could not leave when the rest of the safari left. So he showed up and got ready to depart three days later. He knew the route they were taking, and he knew the destination. He got all his carriers to move in the right direction, and he pushed them to go faster and faster. He was sure if they worked hard enough and pushed hard enough, they could catch up with the rest of the group. On the first day they pushed very hard carrying everything and working their way through the jungle path. They were exhausted, but the next day they started out before daylight and pressed and to catch up to the group. The third day they were getting closer and closer, and they pushed harder than ever. He felt sure the following day would find them overtaking the lead group. He awoke before sunrise and commanded the group to pick up the packs and begin moving. But none of the carriers would get up. He tried everything to get them to move. He offered incentives financially and tried to motivate them emotionally. He even threatened them, but they refused to pick up their packs and go on. He pulled the lead carrier aside to discover what was wrong with the men. The man explained that they were pushed so hard that they were exhausted and that today should be designated as a day of rest. "Today is the day to let soul catch up with body."

So often we don't designate time to let our souls catch up with our bodies. We leave the discipline of rest behind while living life to the full. And we spend all our time working hard, playing hard, studying hard, and serving hard. We need to give equal time and effort into the idea of resting. We need a distraction that gets us away from the stresses and strain of everyday living. We need to learn how to work hard but rest well.

Scientifically early sleep is the highest quality of sleep. Some have proposed that the best sleep that you get is during the time of rapid eye movement and this occurs most often between the hours of 10pm and 2am. What we try to do often in our desire is to get 8 hours of sleep, is to plan to sleep from 12 am to 8am but in reality we might sleep from 12 to 6. So we miss half of that good time of real rest, real dreams, real relaxation, and we age early because of it.

If we are going to be everything we need to be, we've got to have these five areas in balance. Work, play, study, service, and solid rest must all intentionally be kept in balance if we're going to get all we can out of life.

NOTABLE QUOTABLE: "UNLESS A PERSON TAKES CHARGE OF THEM, BOTH WORK AND FREE TIME ARE LIKELY TO BE DISAPPOINTING."
MIKALY CSIKSZENTMIHALYI

DIRECTIVE 13—
STOP RESENTING YOUR PROBLEMS

As a young boy, I grew up watching the various legends of Hercules. I may have watched the entire black and white Hercules series. Naturally, I always marveled at his strength. One of the early episodes of Hercules had to do with his actually developing his great power. In this particular story Hercules was a slave on a row ship and was blessed with the ability to row hard, but because he was a slave on a rowing ship, he would spend hours in the hot sun, pulling and pushing at the oars. This particular legend held his hard work as the secret to his gaining his magnificent strength. It was the problem that he had in being a slave and working so hard in the galley of rowers that caused him to develop his muscles and incredible physical ability.

Scientifically we know that strength is gained by something called Progressive Resistance Exercise (PRE). The idea is to incrementally increase resistance and overload the muscle so that it can grow. In life, strength is also gained by lifting the problems that come your way.

Understand that your problems are individualized. What one person sees as a problem or difficulty another person may not see the same way. It all has to do with your perspective.

In college as I moved from room to room through the years, I always had this quote pinned next to my desk: "Problems, we all know problems. How you handle them makes all the difference in the world. One man gives up, while another one perseveres. And armed with new knowledge borne of trying, he finds a way to succeed. What do you see down a rocky path, stumbling blocks or stepping-stones? It's your point of view that counts."

Recently while I was in South Africa, I ministered to children in Cape Town by way of a game that was new to them called kickball. They understood the concept of baseball, so it helped them understand the basic idea of kickball. While I was explaining the game to them, I watched a barefooted little boy, who couldn't have been more than four years old, bend down and pull out a sharp piece of glass from the bottom of his foot. He removed it, tossed it aside, and got in line so that he could have his turn to kick the ball. One of our young ladies, who was also working with these young children, looked up at me and said, "Did that little boy just pull out a piece of glass from his foot?" When I answered in the affirmative, her eyes rolled, and she shook her head in amazement. We would probably go to the emergency room for a tetanus shot or stitches, but this little boy didn't see it as a problem. He only knew that he didn't want to lose his place in line and that pretty soon he would have the chance to kick the ball and run around the bases. Problems come down to perspectives, and perspectives are individualized.

There is no question that without problems we can't experience progress. Kites rise against the wind not with it. One of the benefits of problems is it can demonstrate to us that we are heading in the right direction. F. D. Meyer writes, "If I am told that the journey is going to be hard while I am on my way getting to the destination, every jolt in the carriage along the road will remind me I'm on the right path."

Problems can also be a pathway to enjoyment. They can help us be grateful for the good things in our lives. As a young boy one of my jobs was to split wood. I recall spending many cold Saturday mornings out in the wood lot, splitting wood by hand. Often times it would rain and be 35 degrees. On more than one occasion my hair would have ice crystals on it. But, I can remember spending four or five hours out there sweating in the cold, seeing my breath, and watching the pile of split wood grow. When I was done, I have great memories of going inside the house and standing in a hot shower for as long as my mother would allow me. Then I would jump into an old pair of sweats, get comfortable in front of a football game, and enjoy some soup and a sandwich. Then I would curl up beneath a blanket and doze in and out of sleep. What great enjoyment that gave me. The hard work in the wood lot let me fully enjoy all of those comforts. Problems also teach you lessons and force you to solve them. They teach other people lessons and how they can solve their own problems. Solving problems not only makes you stronger, but it enables you to face future problems with confidence.

Did you ever consider the problems you have as being the reason why you have a job? Robert R. Updegraff writes: Look for More Troubles:

Be thankful for the troubles of your job. They provide about half your income. Because if it were not for the things that go wrong, the difficult people you have to deal with, and the problems and unpleasantness of your working day, someone could be found to handle your job for half of what you are being paid.

It takes intelligence, resourcefulness, patience, tact, and courage to meet the trouble of any job. That is why you hold your present job. And it may be the reason you aren't holding down an even bigger one. If all of us would start to look for more troubles, and learn to handle them cheerfully and with good judgment, as opportunities rather than irritations, we would find ourselves getting ahead at a surprising rate. For it is a fact that there are plenty of big jobs waiting for men and women who aren't afraid of the trouble connected with them.

A lack of money was one of the problems my family had when I was growing up. Nobody around us had much money either. Like so many young boys, I was compelled to solve this problem on my own. In the summer I would mow lawns and return soda bottles. In the winter I would get up early and shovel snow. What that did for me was to establish a good work ethic that I carry even today. The fact that there was a problem of no money didn't stop me from solving that difficulty and establishing something in my life that would follow me the rest of my days.

Years ago a study was done using an Eco-dome. A giant bubble was built out in the middle of the desert and in it was placed everything necessary to sustain life. There was fresh water, a garden, and livestock for poultry and beef. Also in the Eco-dome was a community of people trying to prove they could live in this environment and life could be easily sustainable. The people lived there month after month. But quickly they learned that the trees supplying the oxygen for the Eco-dome began to die. They found that it wasn't from lack of sunlight because the Eco-dome was transparent and the trees got the proper sunlight. It wasn't due to lack of sufficient water because the water was pumped at just the right level. What they discovered is the trees died because there was no wind. The wind blowing against the trees causes the root system to grow deep, and it also causes the trees to flex back and forth, which helps them to develop the capillaries necessary to bring the water and the nutrients up the trunk to the leaves. The lack of wind caused the death of the trees.

Wind can be seen in our lives as difficulties and the lack of problems may very well cause a lack of growth in our lives. I'm not advocating looking for trouble and causing problems, but we must resist the temptation to see problems as our enemies. William Clement Stone, self help author, put it this way: "So you've got a problem? That's good! Because repeated victories over your problems are the rungs on your ladder to success. With each victory you grow in wisdom, stature, and experience. You become a bigger, better, more successful person each time you meet a problem and tackle and conquer it with a positive mental attitude. Problems can be a great benefit to our life and can be the very thing that gives us the strength to launch our life into a particular area of success."

NOTABLE QUOTABLE: "THE GRINDING OF LIFE CAN BE USED TO SHARPEN YOUR CHARACTER." STEVEN A. JIRGAL

Directive 14—
Make Kind Words Your First Option

Mary sat in my office crying. She came in for counseling because her life seemed to be falling apart. She gave the history of what had gone on in her marriage, with her children, with her friends. She even went further back and explained how bad she felt about herself. Although Mary was approaching fifty, she remembered a time in her life when she was just eleven and her dad gave her a nickname. It was a nickname of derision. It was an attack on her looks, and although this woman was nearly forty years removed from that incident, obviously it scarred her and hurt her deeply. Her father never had a clue regarding the pain that she was carrying.

Our words can be used in so many different ways and so often those words can hurt. It's words that label someone lazy, dumb, or ugly that causes such pain. The fact is, words have the power to help or to hurt, and the tongue can be a dagger that can kill a giant or a balm that can raise the dead.

We all grew up with the adage, "Sticks and stones may break my bones, but names will never hurt me." The person who coined that phrase probably never had words used against him. Words in fact can pierce the heart. They can build you up or tear you apart.

In high school I was a running back on the JV football team. The coach was not very kind. His method of coaching was to ridicule and belittle you, and I got my share of that throughout my sophomore year. I remember one game where we were losing 7-0 at the half. The coach was disgusted with us and brought us to a hillside for adjustments and our half-time motivational speech.

All he said was, "I'm tired of you guys. You figure it out."

Then he walked away and never said another word for the rest of the break. The second half came, and we scored. The clock was running out, and they called my play for a two-point conversion. Everything seemed to go into slow motion as I heard the crowd go crazy. I received the pitch and ran as hard as I could to the corner of the end zone to make the conversion. What a marvelous time in my life! It has been decades later, but I still remember what happened when we returned to school. We showered, and I was one of the last boys to leave the locker room. I was in front of the mirror working on my hair and I remember seeing a figure come out of the coaches' office. I glanced over to see this particular coach approach me. I was nervous. He intimidated me. I didn't know what he would say, and I didn't know what he would do. He tapped me on the shoulder, and as I turned around he took my face in both hands and said, "Nice two points," and then he walked away. Even though so much time has gone by and this was just a small aspect in my life, I carry the look on his face and the words from his mouth with me all these years.

Words make a difference. Kindness has an impact. Words linger in a person's heart, and kind acts last in a person life no matter how much time goes by and no matter how many episodes occur.

I was at a picnic where people were standing around in a large circle. Men and women were eating and talking. Our eyes followed a little girl, a child of one of the adults that was in the circle. We watched her go around the circle and saw the look on her face as she wrapped her arm around the leg of a woman she thought was her mother. She looked up and confusion was pasted across her tiny face. For just a moment she panicked and surveyed the other faces and went running to her mom. The rest of us laughed, but when the laughter ended, the father made a comment about his wife I will never forget. He said, "She should have known that wasn't her mom. That thigh is way too small." There was some nervous chuckling that went on after that, but I looked at that women's face, and I watched her wilt and crumble inside. Words have the opportunity to cut deeply or to build greatly.

We must be willing to commit ourselves to think before we speak. Three questions need to be asked when we have an opportunity to give our opinion and to speak:

-Is it true?

-Is it nice?

-Is it necessary?

If the answer is no to any one of those three questions, then we should take the advice of Will Rogers, "Never miss a good chance to shut up."

In India there is a saying, "When you cut off a man's nose there is no point in giving him a flower to smell." The fact is people tend to gravitate toward an area of kindness. If you want to gather people around as friends you will attract many more people through acts of kindness and words of gentleness than you will by your accomplishments and your wit. It's a kind word, a helping hand, a caring note, or a squeeze of a shoulder that attracts people to your inner circle. Mark Twain said, "I can live three months on a good compliment."

In my office I have a file named "the fuzzy file." Occasionally I will get notes from people who are attempting to encourage me, build me up, and thank me. I don't keep all those notes, but the ones that really hit home with me, the ones that really get me excited, motive me, and encourage me, I put in my fuzzy file. My motivation in doing this is in the understanding that someday when things are not going so well, when I'm at a low point and it seems to be raining all around me, I can grab that file and leaf through it and be built up and motivated to go on by remembering those episodes. The Japanese have a fitting proverb: "One kind word can warm three winter months."

Arguably the greatest compliment you will receive in your life has nothing to do with what an athlete you were, how good a businessperson you were, or the fact that you have been gifted with a particular talent. You'll receive the greatest gift of satisfaction when you learn that those around you see you as having a kind heart.

NOTABLE QUOTABLE: "HAMMERS LEAVE MARKS ON WOOD, FLOWERS LEAVE MARKS ON THE SOUL." STEVEN A. JIRGAL

Directive 15—
Guard Your Reputation

A good reputation may take years to build but can be destroyed in an instant. It's seen in the athlete who throws his helmet, the actress who gets caught in a compromising position, or the businessperson who is found cheating. I have come to learn you can get into more trouble in five minutes than you can work your way out of in a lifetime, and you can't talk your way out of what you behaved yourself into.

Recently two of my favorite athletes fell from the pedestal. Both threatened to kill someone during competition. One said he would break someone's neck. The other threatened to choke someone who was an official at the event. Whether you're a preacher, politician, merchant, manager, farmer, or a father, the higher you go, the bigger the eyes that follow you.

In 1997 Ohio State Trooper Gerald Gibson was honored by MAAD (Mothers Against Drunk Driving) for making the most DWI arrests. However, his pedestal crumbled when in November of 2009 he himself was arrested for drunk driving. Life can change so quickly.

In our area a local coach was also caught with a DWI. He was the man for the job, and he began the season. The players started to get to know him and trust him. But because his past was revealed, his reputation was tarnished, and he can't be hired anywhere in any school district.

Your reputation crumbles at the discovery of your violations. If you understand that, you keep your head on a swivel and remain alert. A friend of mine in ministry shared what happened one day at the beginning of a staff meeting. The meeting started when one of the men said, "Before we go too far, I need to tell you something that has happened in my life. I was driving on my way to an appointment, and I stopped at a red light. In the lane next to me a car pulled up and I could see out of the corner of my eye that the driver was a blond headed young lady. So I looked at her, and she looked back at me. Then she smiled at me, and I smiled back. She held up her hand, and she waved at me, and I waved back. She signaled that I should pull into a parking lot ahead. We started a conversation that was innocent enough. She had a few questions about where she was and needed some directions. She asked who I was and what I did. She was kind, and she was pleasant, and she complimented me. Then she gave me her phone number saying that if I ever needed some help with anything or someone to talk to I could call her. I gave her my phone number and said the same thing. She called me a couple of days later and invited me to lunch, so we had lunch together. We had lunch again another time. Then we had dinner and as things went on we found ourselves in a hotel room. Because of all of this I am going to lose my marriage, family, ministry, and my reputation." Everyone in the room was quiet as they stared at this man in unbelief. Then he said, "Knowing all of those things is why, when she smiled at me, I never smiled back." You could hear a collective sigh of relief in the room. That staff worker understood that it had taken all those years for him to build up a solid reputation. But one episode, one indiscretion, one compromise, and it would all come crumbling down. We have to be very careful to guard our reputations.

The grandparents of a friend of mine always had parting advice for him, "Don't do anything to get your name in the paper." I'm not sure how it was with you, but as children we were charged with never doing anything that would embarrass us, or the family name. It's all about reputation.

NOTABLE QUOTABLE: "A REPUTATION ONCE BROKEN MAY POSSIBLY BE REPAIRED, BUT THE WORLD WILL ALWAYS KEEP THEIR EYES ON THE SPOT WHERE THE CRACK WAS." JOSEPH HALL

DIRECTIVE 16—
PAY THE PRICE FOR GREATNESS

The artist Renoir was inflicted with arthritis, yet he kept on painting. Someone asked him, "Why is it that you keep painting even though you're in such pain?" He said, "The pain is for a moment, but the beauty is for a lifetime." Show me a person who has made it to the top, and I will show you a person with bruises for every step. Don't be surprised by struggles. Sacrifice is a key ingredient to success. You will encounter pits and potholes and barriers all along the road to success. The cost increases with the passion.

Sidney Poitier is a man who wanted to achieve greatness. He wanted to be an actor. He had two things against him: he had a strong Jamaican accent, and he was illiterate. So he had to teach himself to speak differently, and he also had to teach himself to read. Understanding this, with tremendous passion, night after night he would change the way he pronounced his words, and he would read and study. Before long he made it in the acting world, earned numerous awards and gained a star on Hollywood Boulevard.

The world is full of examples of those who have paid the price to be great. It's the athlete who runs one more lap or lifts one more weight, the businessperson whose office light stays on long after the cleaning crew has left, the student who has his nose in the book while his colleagues are busy with entertainment, or the scientist who keeps working for a solution even after his partners has given up and gone after other finds.

Paying the price involves self-denial. It may cost time, energy, money and a host of other natural attractions. Those who are in the pursuit of greatness understand that a moment of glory is worth a lifetime of pain. George Washington Carver had a firm grip on this idea. He had an opportunity to make millions of dollars working for various institutions that recognized his brilliance. But over and over he turned them down so he could work at Tuskegee Institute and develop his theories. Thanks to him we have so many wonderful scientific breakthroughs, many of which simply involved the relentless study of the characteristics and make-up of the peanut. By committing himself to diligent study and continual pursuit of answers, he has been placed in history as one of our greatest scientists.

Years ago a man was asked how he became such a success. He said, "I learned that I could become a success by only working a half a day at a time." Then he finished his thought by saying, "And it really doesn't matter if you work the first twelve hours or the second twelve hours."

Stop daydreaming about the success you'd like to experience someday. Success only comes to those who are willing to commit themselves to hard work. The road to success is never labeled "easy street." Diligence and excellence are the twin sisters of success.

NOTABLE QUOTABLE: "NO MAN CAN BE GREAT UNTIL HE IS WILLING TO HURT HIMSELF DEEPLY." STEVEN A. JIRGAL

DIRECTIVE 17 —
LIVE AN INTENTIONAL LIFE

A man sat on his porch one day, whittling several figures of a horse. A friend came by and noticed what he was doing and asked him how it is that he did such exquisite work. "How do you take an ordinary block of wood and turn it into something as beautiful as the horses that you've made?" The man quietly looked at his friend and simply said, "All I do is cut out anything that isn't horse." That is how we have to live our lives. When we see what it is we are supposed to do, we must live with the intention of achieving that end. Water, if it is focused enough, has the power to cut rocks. Likewise, a sharply focused beam of light can be bounced back and forth between mirrors until it is strong enough to burn through steel.

In the movie *City Slickers*, Billy Crystal plays the part of a businessman who is trying to find his identity. He and two of his friends decide they are going to become short term cowpokes. These city slickers mounted horses and began a cattle drive. Close to the beginning of the movie, Curly, the leader of the cowboys, tells Billy Crystal what he's got to do to find what he is looking for in life. He says, "It's this," and holds up his index finger. At first Billy Crystal doesn't know what that means. But later it clicks with him that there is "one thing." There is one direction, an intentionality to our lives that we have to establish. There is a position that we've got to put ourselves in; in pursuit of that one thing.

The Bible says that Jesus did that. It tells us he set his face steadfastly toward Jerusalem (Luke 9:51). This was the very place where they wanted to kill him earlier. This was the place where a whip would meet his back, and a crown of thorns would be placed on his head. A cross was waiting for him, and he would be killed. But that was his "one thing," that was what he had on his heart and his mind. It was his life focus.

Those in the circus understand the idea of focus. This is particularly important to those who are involved with the flying trapeze. The key to being successful on the flying trapeze is to have complete focus. While the crowd is cheering and you're high up above the earth, while someone is swinging back and forth in front of you and the music's blaring and animals are making noise, you have to close all that out and focus on the person who is supposed to catch you. Then when it's your time to go, there must be no hesitation. You have to swing, focus, let go, and most importantly, you have to catch. There is nothing else on the globe that matters, nothing more, nothing less, nothing else.

A behavioral study was done involving what is called the EQ. The IQ is "Intelligence Quotient." The EQ is the "Emotional Quotient." They placed individual young children all alone in a room. They gave them three M&Ms. The M&Ms were placed on the table right in front of the children, and the children were given these instructions, "If you want, you can eat these M&Ms right now, but that is all you're going to get. But if you wait until I come back, I will give you a whole bag of M&Ms. You can touch the M&Ms, you can roll the M&Ms, you can hold them in your hands, you can do anything you want with the M&Ms, but you can't eat them until I get back." Then the camera rolled, and they watched for the children's reaction. Many of the children couldn't wait. They had to have those M&Ms, so they ate them. But a lot of the children engaged in what's called "Deferred Gratification." They understood, *if I wait now, I will get a greater reward.* So with patience they waited. Then over the years they followed these children as they developed and found that those who had a higher EQ (exercising deferred gratification), succeeded better in school and in relationships.

I have a friend who is very successful in business. I asked him what the secret to his success was and he simply told me, "You have to make a commitment to whatever you're doing. Wherever you are, you must be all there, and whatever job you're doing, you must act like it's the last job you'll have in your life. What he's talking about is focus. It makes the difference between having a little right now and having a lot a little later. Focus and live your life with intention.

NOTABLE QUOTABLE: "THE ONE WHO CHASES TWO RABBITS AT ONE TIME CATCHES NONE." STEVEN A. JIRGAL

DIRECTIVE 18—
TAKE CREDIT FOR WHAT YOU DO RIGHT AND RESPONSIBILITY FOR WHAT YOU DO WRONG

This concept runs contrary to our natural nature. We are naturally driven to defer blame. We are willing to share the blame as long as we're to blame and we can slide it over to somebody else's plate. In this case, perhaps misery does love company. When the possibility of blame comes our way, we are so fearful that somehow we will suffer for our mistakes. The fact is, we are simply fallible, and we will make mistakes-count on it.

Another area that we are concerned with is that of humility. When we do something right, we don't want to come off as somebody who is prideful. Nobody likes a prideful person, and none of us does everything completely on our own. So we must share a compliment when necessary. But for some reason we have the idea that if you simple say thank you when somebody pays you a compliment, then you're being prideful. What you are being is honest.

There are pressures that come from two distinct places in our lives: there is internal pressure and external pressure. Internal pressure is exhibited when we are afraid to let people know we are human. External pressure comes from those who put their expectations upon us that may or may not be realistic. When was the last time you said thank you and let it go when somebody paid you a compliment? Can you recall a time when you said, "I blew it. I was wrong. Forgive me," or "I made a mistake."

In college I was a member of a group of guys who got

together and boxed. Together, we bought some headgear and gloves, and we had a great time sparing with each other and going through the discipline it takes to condition for the sport. After graduation, I hurriedly packed all the gear and took it with me. I completely forgot about it as I dropped boxing from my activities. Years later I was in the garage and opened up a box stored in the back of the closet and found both sets of headgear and both sets of gloves, and I realized I had done something I shouldn't have done. The other guys invested money in this, and yet I was the one who took them home. As time went by, I reasoned that I needed to make this right. Through the alumni office I found out where they were, and I sent each of those men a check and explained to them what I had done, that it wasn't right, and asked for their forgiveness. I received cards back from each of those men saying they had forgotten all about it but really admired me for being open and honest with them and admitting my mistake.

Have you ever been in a meeting when you knew that you had done wrong and made a mistake and simply said, "That one is my fault. I'll take the hit on that one." Too often we take things so personally that when something goes wrong, our first defense is to do damage control and deflect where the blame needs to go. Somehow we won't let other people do that, but we reserve that right ourselves. It's unfair, but we judge everyone else by actions, and we expect to be judged by our intentions. We find it so much easier to take credit for what is right than it is to take responsibility for what is wrong. But we must be willing to accept both. That is simply being honest about life itself.

NOTABLE QUOTABLE: "THE WILLINGNESS TO ACCEPT RESPONSIBILITY FOR ONE'S OWN LIFE IS THE SOURCE FROM WHICH SELF-RESPECT SPRINGS." JOAN DIDION

Directive 19 —
Take Care Of Those Who Can't Take Care Of Themselves

The TV shows that continue to carry great popularity are those who show people helping other people. "Extreme Home Makeover" or "Complete Personal Makeover" are very popular because there is something deep inside us that is drawn to those who help those who can't help themselves. Our hearts melt when we see a picture of a soldier carrying children, a little sister or brother in the Special Olympics, or a very small hand placed in a larger hand. We call them heroes. Unfortunately the problem today is that the pedestals are increasingly empty. We are not supposed to be here to see through each other but rather to see each other through. It's one of the things that help us grow bigger as we travel through life.

Not long ago I heard Dave Sorensen speak. He was one of the people who was labeled a hero in what is now called "The Miracle on the Hudson." A USAir plane had to make an emergency landing in the Hudson River, and as you can imagine, it was sheer chaos inside the cabin. But Dave began yelling instructions and helping people through the rubble and out the door onto the wing. He handed babies to those who could carry them and little children to those who were strong. He was the last person off the airplane that day, and he is held as a hero because he helped so many that couldn't help themselves.

It's a selfless motivation that causes a person to reach down to help those who are less fortunate. Sometimes it's giving a hand out, but most times it's giving a hand up. It is evidenced when a person establishes a scholarship for those who can't afford to go to school. We see it when a couple decides to adopt a young baby from an unfortunate situation. We recognize it when a fireman pulls somebody from a burning building or a medical worker helps somebody in a desperate situation.

Back in the 60s a song was written centering around a picture of young boy carrying his brother with the caption, "He ain't heavy he's my brother." When the world sees somebody helping someone who can't help himself, admiration flows from the heart.

In the fall of 2009, two high school football teams faced each other in St. Joseph Missouri. Benton High School was losing 46-0 with the clock running out. The Benton coach called time-out, and instead of addressing his team, he went across the field to the other coach. He explained to him that he had a boy on his team named Matt Ziesel who had Down syndrome and never played but always practiced. He asked the coach if they would allow the boy to score a touchdown. The two teams lined up, the ball was snapped and Matt, who really didn't understand what was going on, was given the ball and told to run to the goal line. The other team trotted after him faking pursuit while Matt scored a sixty-yard touchdown. That day Matt felt like a hero. That day this boy who couldn't process things well mentally, felt like he was a winner. But even though the team that let him score sacrificed a shut out, they won far more than the scoreboard could ever tell.

NOTABLE QUOTABLE: "A man's worth is measured by how he treats others who can do absolutely nothing for him."
UNKNOWN

DIRECTIVE 20 —
TAKE A CHANCE

When eaglets are learning to fly, the mother will do two distinct things. She will begin bringing sharp branches, pieces of bone, and any other sharp items she can find and line the nest with them. This makes the nest uncomfortable for the little eaglets. She will also nudge them toward the edge of the nest. Then when the moment is just right, she will push that eaglet out of the nest, and he will plummet towards the earth. The mother will then swoop underneath the eaglet and catch it on her back. Then she will climb higher and higher with the little one on her back. In an instant she will turn and drop the eaglet off her back. This will be done over and over again until the eaglet learns not to panic but to fly.

That's the way it is with our lives. We've got to be willing to take a chance. We've got to get uncomfortable in our nest, and we've got to stand on the edge and learn how to soar. You cannot soar until you surrender to the wind.

If you've ever been on a ropes course, undoubtedly you've noticed there are two different sections to the course, the low elements and the high elements. In the high elements area, one of the common pieces of equipment is called the "multi-vine." A multi-vine is a wire that runs from one tree or pole to another with another wire up above. Suspended from the upper wire are several vertical ropes (vines), which are strategically placed far enough apart to force you to let go of one in order to grab the other as you make your way across the wire. You have to abandon the safety of one in order to find safety in the next. It takes courage. It takes you beyond what you normally think you can do.

Life is so much like that. It calls for boldness. You must abandon the safety of the familiar. You have to picture the possibilities, and you have to find your motivation. All mountain climbers know this about climbing. It's a struggle, it's difficult, and there are dangers that are inherit in climbing a mountain. But all of them come to the same conclusion when they defeat the mountain and get to the top: the view is always worth the climb.

Years ago, there was a job opportunity for young boys in a small town. The newspaper was opening a new delivery route, and boys lined up in order to interview for the job. However, there were twenty boys for the one route. One young man in that group was willing to take a chance and do something different from what everybody else was doing. He got there late and was at the back of the line but had so much self-confidence that he was willing to put himself at risk. He quickly wrote something down on a piece of paper and brought it to the front where the man was standing at the door allowing each of the boys to come in and interview for the job. The note simply said, "My name is Jimmy Thomas. Please don't hire anybody until you meet me." He took a chance, and he got the job.

John Schnatter knows what it's like to take a chance and experience the rewards. He enjoyed making food, and he wanted to start a pizza delivery service. He began by working out of a closet in his father's tavern, making pizza for the customers. He wanted to expand, but he had no money. The only thing he had was a 1971 Camaro that he dearly loved. But he made the decision to take a chance and sell his Camaro and with that money started his pizza business. He earned, $1600 dollars for his car, just enough to get his venture off the ground. As he began to work his plan, it grew and grew and today he owns the franchise to over 3,000 pizza stores. We know the pizza delivery service as Papa Johns.

Understandably, taking a chance means different things to different people. If it doesn't involve the possibility of failure, then you're not taking much of a chance. What one person sees as something that is fearful may hold no fear for someone else. The key is to find out what it is you want to do, learn what the risk is, and then be willing to take a chance to make your dream come true.

What will it take for you to gain the motivation that's necessary to move forward and take that chance? Why not give that speech? Why not talk to a stranger, start an adventure, take a class, ask for that raise, take that trip you have always dreamed of, or go out for the team? If you don't take a chance, you are safe, but life is not always meant to be safe. Those who really reach the top and launch their lives into something speculator can always recite to the rest of us the times in their lives where they were scared but took a chance.

NOTABLE QUOTABLE: "HAPPY ARE THOSE WHO DREAM DREAMS AND ARE READY TO PAY THE PRICE TO MAKE THEM COME TRUE."
LEON J. SUENES

DIRECTIVE 21—
DON'T LET ANYTHING BEAT YOU THAT DOESN'T HAVE A HEART

When you're evaluating the obstacles that naturally fall in your path, you have to decide what they are and how they can be defeated. There are lots of obstacles that you are going to encounter as you try to succeed in life. But, the ones that don't have a heart are the ones that you feel worse about when you give in and are defeated by them. It could be a poor attitude, temperature, circumstances, pain, or money. Everybody gets knocked down, but winners find a way to get back up again.

Statistics tell us that the average millionaire goes bankrupt 3.75 times during his career. That means that he faces failure from a financial standpoint. Yet when you look at those peoples' lives, they still are millionaires. It's because they understand that this obstacle called money is not something that they are going to allow to stop them.

Lt. Dieter Dengler was a U.S. Navy pilot during the Vietnam era. He was shot down in 1966 and held captive in a POW camp in Laos. He escaped and spent 23 days evading the enemy, eating anything he could and fighting fatigue and fear. He didn't let hunger, thirst, heat, or fear stop him. He persevered because he had a dream, a desire, and he was pressing himself toward freedom. After being on the run for almost a month, he was rescued and realized the freedom he was looking for.

The key to overcoming obstacles involves evaluating the situation, coming up with a plan, and then enlisting help from those around you. You've got to stick to the plan, double your determination, and just flat out get tough. It starts in your head.

You have to make a decision that no matter what obstacle you come up against, you are not going to let it stop you. No matter what it takes, you're going to press on, push through, persevere and win.

Jesse Owens understood that. He was an amazing track and field athlete from Danville, Alabama. In 1936 he represented the U.S. and traveled to Germany to compete in the Olympic games in Berlin. He faced hatred, Nazism, and bigotry. But all of those things were obstacles that Jesse Owens wouldn't let beat him. They didn't have a heart, and he had a heart that was bigger than his body. By focusing on his purpose, he won four gold medals and defeated bigotry, Nazism, and all the hatred they threw at him. He became a hero to the American people because he refused to be beaten by something that didn't have a heart.

NOTABLE QUOTABLE, "TO QUIT IS TO BE DEFEATED FROM WITHIN."
STEVEN A. JIRGAL

DIRECTIVE 22—
NEVER LET YOUR HEART MAKE MAJOR DECISIONS FOR YOU

A story is told about a man in court who was accused of assaulting his wife. He denied the charges, but as the emotions of the courtroom began to build, the attorney for the woman began to badger him. He asked him question after question, and the emotions went higher and higher. He talked about what the woman said about him again and again in rapid succession. Then finally the man stood up and pointed at the woman and said, "I should have killed you while I had the chance." The court case was over and the judgment went in favor of the woman.

Because of emotions, fights get started, relationships end, regrets are established, and unnecessary items are purchased. In any debate the underlying rule is you must not lose control of your emotions. Even when you are right, if you lose your temper or raise your voice and get emotional, you place yourself in jeopardy of losing. For some people the concept of keeping their emotions out of the decision-making process is very easy. They are "think first" and "feel second" type of people. Other people are wired differently. They are more emotionally bent and "feel first" and "think second." The second group has to be especially careful not to make the mistake of letting their minds take second place to their heart. It is imperative that you think clearly about a decision you've got to make and understand if you're making that decision from the framework of fact or feeling.

Generally, there are five positions people take by way of motivating factors in the decision-making process. I call them the "P factors." Decisions can be based on popularity, position, purse, pride, or principle. Of course decisions made based on principles are the only ones that keep you from making emotional decisions or ones based on improper motivations. David Duford, Personal Trainer writes, "Methods are many, principles are few, methods may vary, but principles never do."

People who are involved in sales love it when a person is an emotional type because there is a good chance a decision will be based on their feelings. Car dealers understand that when a person gains an emotional attachment to a car, the chances of him buying that car are much higher. One of the most difficult positions people can be in is that of planning a funeral for a loved one. They are in a highly emotional state. They've lost someone they dearly love, and they will never get to see that person on this earth ever again. They want to do all the right things, but their decisions tend to be made from an emotional standpoint. They go overboard with flowers, the casket, the entourage, and the limousine. They continually make decisions based on their desire to honor the person. They are making those decisions from their heart and not their head.

Abraham Lincoln tried to avoid making decisions based on emotion. He would often write letters to people that were very direct and strongly worded. Then he would take the letter and place it in a drawer. He would never mail it until he read it again the next day. Often times, however, he never mailed those letters.

To guard against making decisions solely on your emotions, there are some keys that need to be implemented:

-Be careful of making a decision when you're tired.

-Be careful of making a decision quickly. Some have suggested that you need to wait twenty-four hours before making a major decision when your feelings are very much involved.

-Have advisors around you who can see things from a different angle and can make decisions without involving emotions.

NOTABLE QUOTABLE: "DON'T TRUST YOUR FEELINGS; TRUST WHAT YOU KNOW." UNKNOWN

Directive 23 —
Pay Close Attention To Details

So many people live what I would label sloppy lives. They don't know where important things happen to be, they don't show up on time, and they don't have proper financial or heritage records. They go about their lives with the idea that "close enough is good enough." But in so many areas of our lives close enough is not good enough. It calls for exactitude. It calls for attention to detail.

Crime scene investigators understand this. *CSI* is one of the most popular television shows today. One of the reasons why it so popular is they usually solve the crime. Another reason for its popularity is because they pay attention to detail, which is something deep down inside we all wish we could do.

This is also seen in the motion picture industry. When a movie is in production, there is a person hired called the Continuity Director. Because movies are almost always shot out of sequence, this person is in charge of taking pictures as the filming progresses. These pictures are put up on a board because they have to be sure certain things in the previous scene are present in next one. A handkerchief or paper in a pocket must also appear in the next scene. When a person on the street walks into a store, the same signs must be in the window when they exit. If there is a dent in the car when it left one location, the dent has to be there when it arrives in the next location. The movies are full of mistakes where the Continuity Director missed the flow from one scene to another. A mistake by that person becomes glaringly obvious on the big screen. Details count.

There is a large hospital in our city. Obviously a hospital

is a place where you want them to pay attention to detail, especially when it involves your life and your health. But I've noticed something in this particular hospital. They pay attention to even the little things. I have even seen this on the elevator. Everyday the mats on the elevator are changed. The reason why I know they're changed is because it says have a pleasant Monday, Tuesday, Wednesday, whatever day of the week it is. That mat is changed because even those details matter in that hospital.

Recently, I experienced someone's failure in paying attention to detail. I had bought an appliance for my home and had to attach it to the wall. That's when I pulled out all the bolts from the package. I discovered that one of bolts had no threads. Somewhere along the line in the process of assembling that package to be distributed to the customer somebody missed the fact that a shaft on a bolt has to have threads to be useful.

Excellence is proven by attention to details. When a person misses a detail, everyone notices. But a person who takes the time to look at the little things and think through the entire procedure, that person tends to move up the ladder of success.

If you don't happen to be wired for details, then my encouragement to you is work within your strengths and hire to your weakness. Find somebody who's very good at taking care of the little things, the details, and assign them the task of getting the pencils for the meeting you're going to have, the menu for the lunch, or decorations for the social event. If given time most people can think of an unfinished project at home and most of those unfinished projects aren't large projects. They don't require a lot of work to complete them, just a little piece of trim that has to be put back up, some glue for the tile in the bathroom that's supposed to be replaced, the nail for the picture that lays in the corner and hasn't been mounted yet. You've got to do something to motivate yourself to finish the job.

Years ago I learned a secret about painting a house. The secret is to start with the back first. Most people paint their houses because they are concerned about how their house looks from the street. It's all about curb appeal. But if you start in the back, it will do two things. First, you get to work into a routine, and you will perfect your skills at painting. Then when you get to the front, you will do a better job. Secondly, it will force you to finish the job. The truth is, if you start in the front it may delay finishing in the back, but if you start in the back, your goal is to finish in the front and you can see that goal through.

Attention to details can make all the difference in your life. It's what gives you the over-the-top wedding, an edge at work in that presentation, or a higher grade on a particular project in school. All of us are involved in details—some of us take it seriously while others deal with their life in a "close enough" manner. I want to challenge you to pay attention to detail. Do the right thing the right way in the right time and it will make a difference in your life.

NOTABLE QUOTABLE: "EXTRAORDINARY PEOPLE ARE NOT NECESSARILY EXTRAORDINARY BECAUSE THEY DO EXTRAORDINARY THINGS. THEY ARE EXTRAORDINARY BECAUSE THEY DO ORDINARY THINGS EXTRAORDINARILY WELL." STEVEN A. JIRGAL

DIRECTIVE 24—
BE HONEST

In the movie, *Liar, Liar*, Jim Carrey plays the part of Fletcher Reede, an attorney whose entire lifestyle is centered on manipulating the truth in order to get what he wants. He lies in court, in the office, in public, and to his ex-wife and son. He has disappointed his son so often that for his birthday the wish the son makes is that his Dad would just tell the truth for one day. The rest of the movie is played off that wish coming true and displays the struggles he has in being honest. Although it's just a movie, as a society we struggle just as badly with being honest.

Should you doubt that dishonesty is an issue in need of address, consider the following:

-In 2008, retailers lost over $34 billion due to employee theft, shoplifting, administrator fraud, and administrative error.

-An average of 10 million people suffer from identity theft each year. Roughly $1,800 to $14,000 is lost in each of these cases. And it takes between four to six months for the victim to rectify the situation. Identify theft costs businesses an estimated $221 billion each year.

-In 1999 fraud cost the insurance industry an estimated $96.2 billion. More than one-third of people hurt in auto accidents exaggerate their injuries. $54 billion each year is spent on healthcare fraud. Workers' compensation fraud costs the insurance industry $5 billion each year.

Our world is riddled with athletes on steroids, politicians on private payrolls, and men and women who are married but on the move. Whatever happened to honesty? Whatever happened to integrity? Oh, for the days when a man's word was his bond and a handshake meant more than any of today's legal documents.   The illustration is given about a pastor in a small town who had his bicycle stolen. He was struggling over how to find who stole it when a friend gave the suggestion, "You should preach on the Ten Commandments. When you get to the commandment, 'Thou shalt not steal,' overemphasize that. Then look around at the congregation and see who looks guilty." The Preacher thought it was a good idea, and the next Sunday enacted the plan. When the sermon was over, his friend approached him and said, "Pastor, I thought you were going to emphasize 'Thou shalt not steal.' I was surprised that you were so quiet on that point." The Preacher responded, "I know, but as I was delivering my sermon, I thought about the commandment, 'Thou shalt not commit adultery', and that's when I remembered where I left my bicycle." Though we laugh about it, a lack of honesty has infected us on every level from the pulpit to Capital Hill. Josh Billings notes, "As scarce as truth is, the supply has always been in excess of the demand."

The fact is, in no society is dishonesty seen as a virtue. No one likes to be lied to, conned, manipulated, stolen from, or misled. But how do we combat this problem when it is so prevalent in our society? Do we build more prisons? Do we raise the penalty on dishonesty? Do we go public with the names of violators? Though these means may offer some relief from this problem, they are not the complete answer. You and I are the beginning of the answer to it all. We've got to take responsibility for our own personal integrity. "The devil made me do it" never was a good excuse to do a wrong thing.

In order to reign in on the issue of personal honesty, let me suggest five aspects we must deal with.

1. Call it what it is. So often we re-name our behavior in order to soften the offence. But when we deal with other people and issues in a dishonest way, we must call it what it is. "It is a lie, not bending the truth." A little white lie is a big black one that has been whitewashed and resized to fit our desires. It is adultery, not "an affair." If a man or woman will stand before friends, family, their spouse, a minister and Almighty God and give his word and then later break it, then I see no reason why I should believe that they will not break their word to me. It is stealing. It is not "embezzlement." How many things or what price tag do we have to put on the things taken in order for us to label the person taking them a thief?

2. Commit to telling the truth and living the truth. We must stop exaggerating and flat out lying when it comes to information. From golf scores, to travel vouchers, to resumes, we must determine only to tell the truth as it relates to reality. So often we get into trouble because we're trying to either impress others or avoid consequences. Mark Twain said, "When you tell the truth, you don't have to have a good memory."

A group of women was talking about their husband's jobs and what time they got home each evening for supper. One said, "My husband flies in the door at six and wants supper by 6:30." The next one said, "My husband leaves work at five, gets home by 5:15 and wants to eat by 5:30." Another one said, "My husband's faster than all of yours. He works for the government. He leaves work by six, gets home at four, and wants to eat by five." Living truth also involves your "punch-out time" at work.

3. Keep your promises. When you say you're going to be somewhere at a specific time, do everything you can to make that happen. If you promise something, deliver it. People are counting on you. Do your best not to let them down.

Three young boys were busy counting their money. One boy pulled his money out and announced that he had two dimes, a nickel, and three pennies. The second boy said that he had four nickels, a dime, and four pennies. The third boy pulled from his pocket two dimes and one nickel and proclaimed that he had four dimes and a nickel. The others protested saying he only had two dimes. "I have four dimes," he said. "My dad promised me two more dimes when he came home from work today." Keeping your promises in big things and little things really does matter.

4. Understand what's at stake. When you are not living a life of integrity, there are multiple levels of collateral damage that occur. First and foremost, your reputation is checkered. People will quickly learn that you are not a person who can be trusted and few will look to you for areas of responsibility.

Along with that, the integrity of your profession will be put in question. How many jokes have you heard regarding the law, medical, and even the ministerial professions? These are birthed because integrity in those areas is put in jeopardy.

Beyond both of these is the internal damage you do to yourself. The more you compromise in the area of honesty, the easier it becomes to do so again. Rarely do those who steal large sums of money start out taking big amounts. It starts out small. Perhaps a teller personally runs short at the end of the month and slips out a $20 with the intention of paying it back. The next week it becomes a $50, then $100, and before too long the sum grows to an enormous amount. When integrity issues are breached, the tendency is for the infraction to increase both in the amount and the frequency.

There is an old American Indian explanation regarding the conscience. When a person violates his conscience, the heart, which is in the form of a triangle, spins. The corners of this spinning triangle touch the inside of a person causing great internal pain. But when a person is determined to violate their conscience, the heart spins continually, the pain is ignored, and eventually the corners of the triangle shaped heart are knocked off. This is used as an explanation of how someone can repeatedly make choices in violation of conscience.

5. Consider the benefits. Though it's not always easy, when you live a life of integrity, you reap the rewards that follow a life of honesty.

   A. You can be trusted, and you will find people relying on you.

   B. You will be elevated to higher positions of responsibility.

   C. You will be honored by those around you, and your life of integrity will be the subject of conversation both publicly and privately.

   D. You will be worthy of following.

A number of years ago, Readers' Digest carried a story that I think really illustrates the importance of integrity. The article is titled "Catch of a Lifetime."

He was 11 years old and went fishing every chance he got from the dock at his father's cabin on the island in the middle of the lake in New Hampshire. On the day before the bass season opened, he and his father were fishing early in the evening, catching sunfish and perch with worms. Then he tied on a small, silver lure and practiced casting. The lure struck the water and caused colored ripples in the sunset, then silver ripples as the moon rose over the lake. When his pole doubled over, he knew something huge was on the other end. His father watched with admiration as the boy skillfully worked the fish alongside the dock. Finally, he gingerly lifted the exhausted fish from the water. It was the largest one he had ever seen, but it was a bass. The boy and his father looked at the handsome fish gills playing back and forth in the moonlight. The father lit a match and looked at his watch. It was 10 pm – 2 hours before bass season opened. He looked at the fish and then at the boy.

'You'll have to put it back, son,' he said.

'Dad!' cried the boy.

'There will be other fish,' his father said.

'Not as big as this one!' cried the boy.

He looked around the lake. No other fishermen or boats were anywhere around in the moonlight. He looked again at his father, and even though no one had seen them, nor could anyone ever know what time he caught the fish, the boy could tell by the clarity of his father's voice, that the decision was not negotiable. He slowly worked the hook out of the lip of the huge bass and lowered it back into the black water. The creature swished its powerful body and disappeared. The boy suspected that he would never again see such a great fish – at least not in his arms. That was 34 years ago. Today the boy is a successful architect in New York City. His father's cabin is still there on the island in the middle of the lake. He takes his own sons and daughters fishing from the same dock. But he was also right – he never again caught such a magnificent fish as the one he landed that night long ago. But he does see that same fish again and again every time when he comes up *against the question of ethics. For, as his father taught him, ethics are simply matters of right and wrong. It's only the practice of ethics that is difficult.*

Do we do what is right when no one is looking? Do we refuse to cut corners to get the design in on time? Or refuse to trade stocks based on information we know we're not supposed to have? We would if we were taught early in life to put the fish back when we were young. For we would have learned this essential truth-not about how we had a chance to beat the system and took it-but about how dad taught us the right thing, and as a result, we were forever strengthened."

Truth matters, character counts, and although you may not see it in tangible ways, honesty pays.

NOTABLE QUOTABLE: "YOU ARE ALREADY A CONSEQUENCE IN THE WORLD IF YOU ARE KNOWN AS A MAN OF STRICT INTEGRITY. IF YOU CAN BE ABSOLUTELY RELIED UPON, IF WHEN YOU SAY A THING IS SO, IT IS SO, IF WHEN YOU SAY YOU WILL DO A THING, YOU DO IT, THEN YOU CARRY WITH YOU A PASSPORT TO UNIVERSAL ESTEEM." GRENVILLE KLEISER

Directive 25—
Live Your Life With The End In Mind

Most people don't like to talk about end of life issues. They don't want to consider the fact that their life is going to end someday. It's not pleasant, it's not normal, and it's not natural. But the fact is no one here gets out alive. Someday you and I will pass from this earth. All roads truly do lead to the cemetery. Because of my job I am involved in a lot of funeral preparations. Some funerals are a celebration of a life well lived, but in all honesty some of them have an undercurrent of regret.

When you die, people will be talking about you. Your life will be brought up, and they will say things publicly that may be different from what they say privately. Our goal should be that the positive things people are willing to say privately, they are also willing to say publicly.

There are two categories of questions it is helpful to ask ourselves regarding our lives and our upcoming funeral. The first question is, "What will people say about me?" Whether you know it or not, you are currently preaching your own funeral. How you deal with people and how you deal with life is going to be reflective in what they say about you both publicly and privately upon your passing.

The words to this poem from an unknown author reflect well what our attitude should be regarding the life we are living and the legacy we are leaving.

It is paramount that you invest your life in something and someone beyond yourself. You must have something that you've stood for and you must have someone you stood by.

While in a hotel lobby, I struck up a conversation with a

man named Harry. He was from Australia and was quick to share with me some insight regarding how we should live our lives. Among other things, he recited from memory a poem written by Edmund Vance Cooke:

How Did You Die?

Did you tackle the trouble that came your way
With a resolute heart and cheerful?
Or hide your face from the light of day
With a craven soul and fearful?
Oh, a trouble's a ton, or a trouble's an ounce,
Or a trouble is what you make it.
And it isn't the fact that you're hurt that counts,
But only how did you take it?

You are beaten to earth?
Well, well, what's that?
Come up with a smiling face.
It's nothing against you to fall down flat,
But to lie there—that's disgrace.
The harder you're thrown, why the higher you bounce;

Be proud of your blacken eye!
It isn't the fact that you're licked that counts;
It's how did you fight and why?

And though you be done to death, what then?
If you battle the best you could;
If you played your part in the world of men,
Why, the Critic will call it good.
Death comes with a crawl, or comes with a pounce,
And whether he's slow or spry,
It isn't the fact that you're dead that counts,
But only, how did you die?

When you set your life up the right way, people do not hesitate to say good things about you after your passing.

The second compelling question you must ask is, "What will God say about me?" Life is more than just giving off a few BTU's and exchanging oxygen for CO_2. When you and I die we will be standing in front of a judge. Our entire life has been a preparation for that meeting. What we will discover at that moment is that everyone lives forever but not everyone lives forever in the same place. I fully recognize that some people don't believe in God while others have lined their life up with what they believe to be God's plan. From the philosophical standpoint it can be clearly seen that if you believe in God and you're right, you gain everything. If you believe in God and you're wrong, you lose nothing. If you don't believe in God and you're right, you gain nothing. If you don't believe in God and you're wrong, you lose everything.

The key in life is to line your life up with God's great plan for you. There are three things I believe God is going to address when our lives are judged at our passing:

1. *What did you do with your time?* All of us have different measures of time that we have been allotted on earth. Did we make the most of our time? Did we take the time and invest it in godly things and in people's lives?

2. *What did you do with your talent?* Different people have varying amounts of talent. God has given us those talents so that they can be used. Did we use them effectively?

3. *What did you do with my son Jesus Christ?* Everyone chooses to be a follower of someone. You can choose to be a follower of yourself and your own desires, or you can elect to be a follower of someone else, but everyone finds himself in a position of following someone or something. Who you follow at that moment will be the only thing that matters for all eternity.

Please understand this: God loves you. He is not mad at you. He is not necessarily happy with some of the things you have done, but He is not mad at you. In fact, He shows how much he loves you, and He wants to spend all of eternity with you, so much so that He was willing to die to make that happen.

A lot of people are afraid of having a relationship with

God Almighty because they are afraid they will have to give up so much of the things they enjoy in life. This is true. Some of the habits and some of the behaviors have to be given up if you're really going to be a follower of God. But in essence what God wants us to give up are the things that hurt us physically, the things that hurt us emotionally, and the phoniness inside. That's an exchange that will make all the difference in each person's life for all eternity.

NOTABLE QUOTABLE: "A RELATIONSHIP WITH GOD MEANS THAT HE GETS ALL THE GLORY AND YOU GET ALL THE BLESSINGS."
STEVEN A. JIRGAL

About the Author

Dr. Jirgal is a 1980 graduate of Gettysburg College where he became a four-time conference champion and All-American in the pole vault. He holds an undergraduate degree in health education and physical education. Following graduation, he taught on the high school and college level while coaching football and track in both venues. He holds Masters degrees in health education, sports medicine, and divinity, as well as a doctorate in ministry.

He has been an area director for the Fellowship of Christian Athletes and has served on the staff of Hickory Grove Baptist Church in Charlotte, NC. Currently he is the Senior Pastor of Lakeview Baptist Church, in Monroe, NC.

Dr. Jirgal serves on the local board of directors for the Fellowship of Christian Athletes, The Carolina Study Center, and the Fathers in Touch ministry. He is also a member of the board of trustees for New Orleans Seminary as well as the ministerial board of Wingate University.

Dr. Jirgal is the chaplain for Sports Spectrum magazine.

He and his wife Pam have three children, Joshua, Caleb, and Sarah. They reside in Monroe, NC.

To view other publications by Dr. Steve Jirgal, go to www.stevejirgal.com.

To schedule a Forerunners inc. presentation for your business or organization go to www.stevejirgal.com or call 704-219-5220.

LIFE POINTS is a project of Forerunners Inc. No information may be copied or used for any reason without the expressed written consent of the author.

ADDITIONAL BOOKS BY

Price: $25.00
118 pages

Silver Anniversary Edition:
Celebrating 25 Years of Sports & Faith

An inspiring book that tells the faith stories of the most prominent Christian sports figures who have appeared in the pages of Sports Spectrum magazine the last 25 years.

Called by some the Christian Sports Illustrated because of its design and quality, Sports Spectrum has interviewed the superstars in the Big Four (NFL, Major League Baseball, NBA and NHL) as well as stars in speedskating, surfing, skateboarding, rodeo, bull riding, and other sports.

Like the magazine, these stories will inspire you in your faith or cause you to examine your life to see if Christ is a part of it.

Price: $14.95
106 pages

Drive Thru Success:
Finding Success While Waiting in the Drive Thru

Looking to live a successful life? Then take a seat and join the ride in Drive Thru Success, by Robert B. Walker - a successful pro sports agent for more than 20 years who uses the drive thru experience as an illustration for finding true success in life. Each step of the drive thru experience represents a different step for success. Everyone has been through a drive thru, so let's learn from it. Learn about life's choices at the drive thru menu. Learn about patience while sitting in line. Learn about trust while getting your order. Drive Thru Success is a great read for everyone of any age who is searching to achieve success in business, athletics, school, and life. So what are you waiting for? Jump in!

Price: $14.95
106 pages

Life Points:
25 Directives That Will Change the Way You Live

Whether you're a businessperson, parent, student, or athlete, life can be confusing. If you don't have the information you want, it can be frustrating. But if you don't have the direction you need, it can be devastating. Life Points has been written to add the directives needed to set your life on a course of success. Among other things, by implementing the individual directives, you'll learn the importance of: Surrounding yourself with the right people; that personal freedom comes from personal discipline; choosing your battles; living a balanced life; taking chances ... and so much more. By systematically following the book's directives, you will have the motivation, information, and plans to accomplish so much more in your life. Life Points will give you the foundation you need to launch your life in a direction that will be fulfilling, exciting, and successful.

To order the books above 1•866•821•2971 or visit our website at www.sportsspectrum.com

Training Table:
10 For 10 Sports Devotionals For the Seasons Within the Season

The Core Media Group, Inc., and Sports Spectrum magazine present Training Table: 10 for 10 - Sports Devotionals for the Seasons Within the Season, is a devotional book for athletes, coaches and sports fans.

Price: $12.95
140 pages

This is a unique tool to further the development and spiritual growth of individuals. Sports analogies can teach valuable truths about life as revealed through the truth of the Bible. Training Table: 10 for 10 provides 10 devotionals for 10 topics that provide a truth or biblical principle to apply to your daily life and sporting life.

Wisdom and Sports
Sports Devotionals and Sports Stories Based on the Book of Proverbs

Verses from all 31 chapters of Proverbs are paired with spiritually encouraging stories of well-known athletes and thought-provoking devotionals. You will be inspired as you read each page of this book written by Robert B. Walker.

Living the Thankful Life

Living the Thankful Life includes 30 short stories about things that Robert is thankful. It also includes an area to write your own stories of thanks, which enables you to make it a legacy book for you, your family and others concerning living a thankful life.

COMING 2011

Cultivating the godly Athlete:
Our Faith On and Off the Field
[Coming 2011]

Twenty biblical qualities for the spiritual development of athletes on and off the field. This is an in-depth look at what faith on the field looks like, and how our lives as Christians are to be mirrored in all of our endeavors in life including sports.

CPSIA information can be obtained at www.ICGtesting.com
Printed in the USA
BVOW010051040112

279596BV00004B/2/P